Imagine My Surprise . . .

Imagine My Surprise . . .

Unpublished Letters to

The Daily Telegraph

EDITED BY

IAIN HOLLINGSHEAD

First published 2012 by
Aurum Press Limited
7 Greenland Street
London NW1 0ND
www.aurumpress.co.uk

A catalogue record for this book
is available from the British Library.

ISBN 978 1 78131 019 9

10 9 8 7 6 5 4 3 2 1
2016 2015 2014 2013 2012

Typeset in Mrs Eaves by SX Composing DTP, Rayleigh, Essex
Printed in Great Britain by Clays Ltd, St Ives plc

SIR – As well as several helpings of pudding, I tucked into the third instalment of unpublished letters over Christmas. Yet again, it was witty, insightful and, in many cases, rude. I found it best served with the fire on, the children in bed, and a dram or four of single malt. I look forward to volume four.

Incidentally, does the paper keep a record of how many letters individuals have had published? It would be interesting to see where I fit in the league table.

Andrew Holgate
Woodley, Cheshire

SIR – Might I suggest that in future editions you add an index so that the more conceited among us can rapidly see if we have made the book? Is there anything more humiliating than to discover that not only have one's efforts failed to make publication in the newspaper, but they cannot even make the book of rejects?

Robert Lightband
Dundee

SIR – It seems rather strange that, with Europe in crisis and the Greek people relying on outside humanitarian aid, anyone would enter into correspondence about lavender-scented bath towels.

M.J. Annett
Burstow, Surrey

CONTENTS

CONTENTS

INTRODUCTION

Last Christmas, when we published *I Rest My Case . . .*, the third in the series of unpublished letters to *The Daily Telegraph*, some people expressed their concerns about the seeming finality of the book's title. Could an eventful year in which London burned, the Middle East revolted, Prince William wed, bin Laden died, Nick Clegg cried and Silvio Berlusconi bunga bunga-ed be our readers' last hurrah?

Fie! Our wonderful readers, choleric, trenchant, wise, witty, waggish, and often downright outrageous, are made of sterner stuff. We've been fortunate in that this year has been no less eventful than last. You might have noticed the Olympics, the Diamond Jubilee, the Eurozone crisis, the endless rain . . . 2012 has been the year of Andy Murray and Jessica Ennis, Rebekah Brooks and Abu Qatada, hosepipe bans and droughts, pasties and jerry cans. Dave chillaxed. Boris bumbled his way to another victory. And Pippa Middleton maintained her place in the heart of the picture editor, if not those of the readers.

Great events alone do not, of course, make for great correspondence. Only *Telegraph* letter-writers are capable of merging the weighty, the whimsical and the quotidian to such hilarious advantage. The water companies impose a hosepipe ban; a reader wonders if he can irrigate his lawn by staging a domestic riot and drawing fire from the police's water cannon. England are knocked out in the quarter-finals of Euro 2012; a reader wonders if the team's copious tattoos are sapping the strength of their muscles underneath. The chief executive of RBS rejects his enormous bonus; a reader writes to say that he doesn't mind him keeping it, as long as he spends £1,000 replacing his 'disgracefully cheapo' pair of hunting boots.

If you look for stereotypical *Telegraph* letter-writers in these pages, you will no doubt find them. One correspondent admits that, if there were a political party for the Disgusted of Tunbridge Wells, she would be one of the first to join. Recurring themes emerge year on year, whether complaints about Andy Murray's facial hair (Robert Jay QC is a new entry in this category this year), the proliferation of retired colonels on the letters page, the crossword, the Americanisation of the English language, the BBC, the EU, wind farms or the sinking sartorial standards among the population at large. All are delivered with customary aplomb, not to mention a deliciously, devilishly erudite turn of phrase.

More surprising, perhaps, is the sheer range of correspondents, their remarkable generosity of spirit and their continual ability to surprise and delight. This year features everyone from a 13-year-old boy pointing out ornithological mistakes in the television adaptation of *Birdsong* to a sexagenarian trying to keep his wife away from the alarming news that 67 per cent of women over the age of 80 are sexually active. One of my favourites comes from a pensioner in North Yorkshire who started watching the televised Jubilee concert in no mood for 'pop' artists and, several bottles of wine later, ended up 'dancing the night away in a modernistic style' with his wife.

I hope you enjoy spending time with our readers as much as I do every year, following the conversation as it echoes, sometimes answered, sometimes ignored, from Piddletrenthide in Dorset to Durness-by-Lairg in Sutherland, via Llanfairfechan in Conwy, Goodworth Clatford in Hampshire and, occasionally, Bessines-sur-Gartempe in Limousin, France.

To all our correspondents, my grateful thanks — as well as to Christopher Howse, the letters editor; Matt Pritchett; Caroline Buckland; and everyone at Aurum. I am particularly grateful to Guy Stagg, who did a huge amount of invaluable work sifting through the letters as they came in and rescuing the unpublished gems from the slush pile.

I'm already looking forward to doing it all over again next year — just as long as we don't run out of titles.

Iain Hollingshead
London SW1
August 2012

FAMILY
LIFE AND
TRIBULATIONS

FROM SHEFFIELD, WITH LOVE

SIR — At the risk of making a sweeping generalisation, why are men so inept when it comes to buying gifts?

On Christmas morning my husband presented me with a set of stainless steel cutlery, a not entirely welcome addition to the five sets I already possess. While this latest attempt at a romantic gesture is a slight improvement on the exercise machine debacle of a few birthdays ago (for which he is still paying), as long as there are men like my husband around, the burghers of Sheffield can rest easily in their beds.

Most galling of all, the kitchenware shop is directly opposite my favourite jeweller's.

Louise Thistlethwaite
Askam-in-Furness, Cumbria

FOLIE A QUATRE

SIR — Your letter-writer admits that he and his partner often talk in a faux Lancashire accent and asks, 'Is this lunacy common?' Not only do my husband and I speak to each other in accents ranging from Valleys Welsh (he's English, I'm Scottish) to broad Yorkshire, we also have a coded language which only we understand, and we frequently dance around the kitchen in our underwear.

We are of the firm belief that if we were ever to be

observed while home alone, we would promptly be
thrown in the loony bin.

S. Frances King
Ashford, Kent

SIR – This morning, in time-honoured tradition,
I woke my husband with a cup of tea and 'a pinch
and a punch on the first day of the month, and no
returns', followed by 'a sock in the eye for being so
sly'.

I wonder: do the kids of today continue to do
this? Unlikely.

Janet Turner
Frome, Somerset

SIR – If one of us is having a lie-in, the signal that
we are awake is given with two sharp coughs so that
a tea-tray can be delivered. I thought we were a bit
quirky until we stayed with friends this weekend and
discovered that they have a similar system – only they
send a text message.

Shirley Batten-Smith
Watford, Hertfordshire

TILL HOUSEWORK US DO PART

SIR – A survey reported last week found that men are more content the more housework they do. This week it was reported that men are more likely to divorce the more housework they do.

I assume, therefore, that divorced men with clean and tidy homes are the most content.

Stephen Sharp
Netherwitton, Northumberland

SIR – Is there, I wonder, any significance as to which side of the matrimonial bed one occupies? A short survey carried out recently by me can find none, other than to confirm that once the decision is made it becomes fixed for the duration.

Tom Whitmore
Southwell, Nottinghamshire

SIR – My advice for a man looking for a wife who will love him unconditionally: claim that you are infertile and have poor career prospects.

Mervyn Vallance
Great Totham, Essex

SIR — Marriage cannot be taught; it can only be learned through trial and error. It's always a trial and often an error.

Mark Taha
London SE26

A GAY ANNIVERSARY

SIR — My wife and I recently celebrated 50 years of happy, even gay, marriage. However, we remain steadfastly heterosexual and untempted by other choices. Will this soon become illegal?

Richard Shervington
Stansted, Essex

SIR — If 'marriage' is to have a new meaning imposed upon it, might it be possible for 'gay' to recover its original meaning?

Rev. Graham F. Perryman
Frome Vauchurch, Dorset

SIR — I am wondering how much redefining of the word 'marriage' is going to cost prospective couples. Labelling goods as 'organic' has certainly caused an increase in their price.

J. Alan Bibby
Eccleston, Lancashire

A FRIEND IN DOROTHY

SIR – Back in the 1950s, as an earnest young man, I attended a tea dance at the Dorothy Café in Cambridge. I was making extremely heavy weather with my partner when another couple pirouetted past us, dancing superbly. As they gyrated, I heard the man ask his partner, 'And what do you think was the cause of the downfall of the Byzantine Empire?'

Desperate for the answer, I pushed my partner to keep station, but lost them as they twirled expertly away from us.

I blame all my subsequent failures in life on not having the answer revealed.

Nigel Thomas
Elham, Kent

NOT PG RATED

SIR – I read that they're going to eroticise *Jane Eyre* to reflect the times. How soon before P.G. Wodehouse gets the same treatment?

Sammy Noe
London NW11

SIR — *Fifty Shades of Grey* — succinctly describes my lingerie collection.

Deb Carroll
Stockport

SIR — Having read the article 'How e-books made reading sexy again', I am at a loss to understand the connection between the relaxing, mind-engaging process of reading and the purely physical and turbulent activity of sex.

The only connection I can find is the feeling of irritation when either process is interrupted.

I hate to feel I am missing something.

Pam Stark
Hadleigh, Essex

THE DAILY GRIND

SIR — We are led to understand that, following a study, a gynaecologist in Florida has confirmed the anatomic existence of the elusive G-spot. If that is his work, I wonder what he does for pleasure.

Mike Rafferty
Winchcombe, Gloucestershire

SIR – My wife's G-spot is centred on the manager's special rail in a well-known high street clothing store.

Alan Beer
Staines, Surrey

SIR – You report that one third of women would prefer weight loss to a night of passion. Have they not considered that the latter might help them to achieve the former?

Ted Shorter
Hildenborough, Kent

SIR – You report that a man has been seen in a yodelling outfit – aka lederhosen – in a nature reserve in Hertfordshire, apparently looking for illicit sex. In August 2010 I walked the entire length of the King Ludwig Way in Bavaria in my lederhosen and no one approached me with the offer of a sexual encounter.

This summer I was planning to go to Italy, but Hertfordshire now looks a more promising destination.

Charles White
Washingborough, Lincolnshire

SIR – When I read this story, it brought to mind something similar that happened to my mother and me many years ago.

We were walking along the banks of the local river when we saw a man coming towards us, wearing nothing but boots. He asked the time. My mother, without any hesitation, replied, 'Oh dear. Have you forgotten your watch?'

Anne Robinson
Collingham, West Yorkshire

SIR — It is bad enough reading that Colin Firth's wife has dispensed with her underwear, but to publish the fact that 67 per cent of women over 80 are sexually active and that most achieve orgasm is devastating news.

Are you mad, sir? I am a mere male (not a rampant young stud) of 68 years, still trying to live up to some vague sexual expectations. Not being certain whether or not I have succeeded is bad enough, but the thought of perhaps another two decades of strenuous and possibly gymnastic marital duties is just too much.

My only resort is to prevent my wife from reading *The Daily Telegraph*.

Geoff Milburn
Glossop, Derbyshire

SIR — With whom do these lusty superannuated ladies indulge their desires? It is most unlikely that gentlemen of 80 could perform the necessary function. The conclusion must be that the task is delegated to younger gentlemen, perhaps of the toy boy persuasion.

Bill Williams
London N7

FRENCH KISSING

SIR – In France, both men and women greet each other with a handshake and a kiss. The kiss is without contact and inaudible.

In this country, over the last decade, the greeting seems to have been mimicked with the addition of a loud 'Mwah' or similar noisy expression. How on earth has this bizarre practice developed?

Chris Harding
Parkstone, Dorset

SIR – How is a man to know whether one kiss is expected without offering the second? Can't we just go back to the single kiss?

Michael Powell
Tealby, Lincolnshire

VEG AND TWO MEATS

SIR – Your report entitled, 'Lamb curries that
miss the vital ingredient . . . some lamb' reminded
me of a menu I saw in a fairly downmarket Indian
restaurant years ago. 'Meat curry: £3.50; Meat curry
(named meat): £3.80'.

Anya Spackman
Watton-at-Stone, Hertfordshire

SIR – Rowan Pelling's tales of her curmudgeonly
father reminded me of a pub I visited in Derbyshire
some years ago. The landlord kindly declined to
pour me a pint of my chosen beer on the grounds
that, 'If yer not used to it, it'll gi' yer the runs.'

He then turned to a rather superior tweedy chap
who asked for a Campari.

'No Campari.'

'A Dubonnet, then?'

'No Dubonnet. I'll gi' yer a gin and tonic.'

Mr Tweedy protested that he didn't want a gin
and tonic and was fixed with a beady eye.

'This is Youlgreave. Yer'll get what yer given.'

Trish Sheldon
Newcastle-upon-Tyne

SIR – Due to an acute shortage of babysitters, our
granddaughter became accustomed to restaurants at a
fairly early age. When asked one evening, aged three,

what she would like to eat, she replied, 'Pâté de foie gras, please, and peas.'

A. Latus
Long Riston, East Yorkshire

SIR – While the debate on breastfeeding in public runs on, it is also a natural thing to need the lavatory when dining out, but would one do it at the table?

Cynthia Walton
Dryslwyn, Carmarthenshire

IMPERIAL RICE

SIR – While clearing out her late mother's larder last week my wife came across an unopened packet of Vesta Beef Curry with rice, priced at three shillings. This would make it at least 40 years old.

K.C.
Hurst, Berkshire

SIR – Your correspondent notices that a pickled onion cost him eight shillings. I gave up converting prices into old money when I realised that it now costs six shillings to spend a penny.

Grant Goodlad
Thornby, Northamptonshire

SIR – Your correspondent's letter reminded me of my father, who regularly ate large quantities of raw onion, accompanied by tea without milk. After giving up smoking roll-ups, Dad also had to shave the end of his nose daily and could unfailingly light his own farts – possibly the result of eating all those raw onions.

Not surprisingly, he was my hero and I still miss him.

Bruce Denness
Whitwell, Isle of Wight

A CHEEK FOR A CHEEK

SIR – Despite what a professor says on your letters page today, I still think a tap on the backside has its merits.

When I was a 10-year-old pupil at a school in Surrey, the deputy head teacher smacked me on the face – allegedly for cheek. My reply was to hit him back and run as fast as I could to the nearest bus stop.

Years later, I decided to admonish my 12-year-old son by challenging him to a wrestling match. I ended up on the kitchen floor, much to my wife's horror.

Richard White
Harpenden, Hertfordshire

SIR – When my sons were at prep school the ultimate punishment for bad behaviour was the gym shoe. One year the headmaster decided, as an experiment, not to use it for a term. When I asked him how it had gone, he replied that the children's behaviour had been markedly worse. The next term the gym shoe was reinstated.

When he retired, the headmaster donated it to the boy who had received it the most times in his final year.

Elisabeth Larpent
Piddletrenthide, Dorset

SIR – You report a letter by Roger Griffin, a school teacher, given as evidence to a disciplinary panel, in which he writes: 'If they (children) don't like being called idiots, fools, clowns, buffoons or any similar epithet, there is a very simple solution: don't act like one.'

Thank you, Mr Griffin, for this ray of realism. It brought back tears and warm nostalgic memories of my own school days.

Philip Hodgkins
Grosmont, Monmouthshire

A CAPPUCCINO FOR PERSEPHONE

SIR – When the staff at Starbucks started asking my name to personalise my take-away cup, I must admit I thought it was a cheesy promotion. However, I never realised quite how much fun it would be. Over the last month I have been, amongst others, Araminta, Chardonnay, Genevieve, Consuela and Antoinette.

Although it probably doesn't say much about my life, the call of 'A cappuccino for Persephone' makes me smile on a rainy day.

Jo Marchington
Ashtead, Surrey

A NON-U FRIDGE

SIR – My ingrained snobbery – along with the service, quality, guarantee etc. – led me to order my new fridge-freezer from John Lewis. Imagine how I felt when instead of a green van with the John Lewis logo, my neighbours saw a U-Drive van roll up.

I have written to the chairman to complain.

R.S. Valentine
Devizes, Wiltshire

TRENDY GARDENING

SIR – Beware the Chelsea Flower Show effect. When I complimented a friend on her trendy wildflower border recently, she replied somewhat icily that she had not got round to clearing it yet this year.

Meryl Parker
Harlington, Bedfordshire

SIR – I have tried everything to keep badgers out of my garden and have at last, I think, found the answer. For 10 nights I played Radio 4 in the middle of the lawn. Yesterday I removed the radio, cut the grass and there was not one badger digging. Unfortunately, squirrels must be deaf.

Alan Webb
Stratton-on-the-Fosse, Somerset

GETTING ROUND THE HOSEPIPE BAN

SIR – During the hosepipe ban, will it be legal for me to hold my power-shower head out of the bathroom window, or will that be considered a 'hose by another name'?

George Sizeland
Carterton, Oxfordshire

SIR – I see that the police may be given powers to use water cannon to quell any rioters this summer. If one staged a riot on one's lawn, could one get it watered?

> **R.W.**
> Castle Rising, Norfolk

SIR – I was informed this morning – by someone who has extensive underground watering in the garden of their mansion – that if I get a hot nail, make lots of holes in the hosepipe and lay it just beneath the soil, I am allowed to run it day and night.

> **D. Phillips**
> Marlborough, Wiltshire

SIR – You report that 'half of sports pitches may turn to dust' because of an impending drought. Judging by what I have seen of modern sportsmen, there should be enough spittle to keep the pitches green all summer.

> **Dennis Graves**
> Crowborough, East Sussex

SIR — Even if there was no drought I would welcome water from Scotland piped south, especially from the Borders where I grew up, as it is very tasty.

Even after 17 years I am still not partial to furry water.

Ginny Hudson
Swanmore, Hampshire

CAN WE HAVE OUR DROUGHT BACK, PLEASE?

SIR — Is this the wettest drought since records began?

Simon Perks
Headcorn, Kent

SIR — If I hear one more water company spokesman say that the rain has made no difference to water levels, I will personally drown him in the lake which used to be my garden.

Sandy Pratt
Lingfield, Surrey

SIR — Having taken the advice of experts, I have recently finished replanting my garden with Mediterranean, drought-resistant plants. However, my garden now resembles a paddy field. Would the best way forward be to plant rice and perhaps use this as a cash crop?

Adrian Dingle
Corsham, Wiltshire

SIR – I bought a rather beautiful straw sun hat in early June. It has rained every day since. Did I do something to irritate the gods?

Claire McCombie
Lower Ufford, Suffolk

SIR – A few weeks ago Caroline Spelman, the Secretary of State for the Environment, announced that there was a drought. Since then we have had little else but torrential rain. Perhaps she should be transferred to the Treasury, where she can point out that we are broke.

Ted Shorter
Hildenborough, Kent

SIR – I think it's time we jumped on the bandwagon and asked the rest of Europe to bail us out.

Phil Merivale
Keyhaven, Hampshire

SIR – I wonder if, by running the Hadron Collider in the opposite direction, the jet stream might be blasted off its current trajectory.

Roger Fowler
Chipping Campden, Gloucestershire

SIR – At a wedding I attended on Saturday there was a reading from Solomon's *Song of Songs*: 'See! The winter is past; the rains are over and gone . . .' – at which point the congregation roared with laughter.

Simon Jarvis
Seaview, Isle of Wight

SIR – Heard on the weather forecast on Radio 4 this morning: 'Good spells of not raining'.

Rosemary Eustace
Coombe Green, Worcestershire

SIR – It's 5 June and you can tell summer's over; the butter's gone hard.

John Rowlands
Harpenden, Hertfordshire

SIR — For the first time in 58 years, I had to put a hot water bottle in my wife's side of the bed on midsummer night.

Roderick Taylor
Bourne End, Buckinghamshire

SIR — How long does this atrocious weather have to last before pensioners can claim a summer heating allowance?

Joyce Chadwick
Stratford-upon-Avon, Warwickshire

SIR — We moved to Chiddingfold in December last year, partly on the assurance that 'some parts of the South East of England get less rain than the Middle East'. Which parts?

Michael Chesterman
Chiddingfold, Surrey

SIR — We have had two days of sunshine, with some more forecast. Does this mean that we may expect another hosepipe ban?

Tore Fauske
Woodmancote, Gloucestershire

EQUINE POOP SCOOP

SIR — The other day my daughter asked me why it was that, although dog owners are now expected to clean up after their animals, the same does not seem to apply to horse owners. As we stepped around another large, steaming pile, I found myself stumped for an answer. Any ideas, horse owners?

Anne Carrington
Bridgeyate, Gloucestershire

SIR — Having retired as a working gun dog to a life indoors, our springer spaniel Gemma would often watch television. One day, shortly before Christmas, when The Famous Grouse was running its advertisement, Gemma was awakened from her slumbers by the distinctive 'go-back, go-back' call. She studiously watched the remainder of the advert, which obviously brought back happy memories, and when it finished she went behind the television to try to effect what would have been her best retrieve ever.

D.F.
Upholland, Lancashire

SIR — As a regular visitor to the UK, I have been fascinated by the spate of letters regarding the television viewing of assorted pets. They have reinforced my view that the British are quite, quite mad.

Long may it be so.

John Eagle
Norwich

ROYAL MALE

SIR – I live in the middle of an historic village. When a Post Office official came to slap some paint on the letterbox in the wall of my house, he said that he couldn't paint the letters gold because the Post Office was cutting back.

That night I sent my husband out, disguised in a balaclava, to touch it up with a tin of gold (this is just one of many subversive jobs I give him to keep him busy). I now get great satisfaction out of seeing visitors photographing the post box.

Caroline Binley
Geddington, Northamptonshire

SIR – Despite the announcement that the prices of postage stamps are to increase dramatically, my wife and I wish it to be known that we shall still be sending Christmas cards to all our friends this year. Without stamps.

Ian Wade
Harlington, Bedfordshire

SIR – On 29 March I bought 1,000 second-class stamps at a cost of £360. I calculate my future saving to be £170. Can anyone suggest where I could obtain a better return on my money?

David J. Filsell
Coombe, Surrey

COLD-SHOULDERING THE COLD CALLERS

SIR – How do other readers fob off the sales callers who seem so expert at interrupting one's food? Tonight an Asian gentleman told me that he wished my valued opinion about something. I informed him that I didn't have a valued opinion, and that he obviously did not know my wife, who has told me for years that no one is the slightest bit interested in what I think.

W.M.
Tiverton, Devon

SIR – When I was in practice as a solicitor, I used to deal with cold callers by interrupting them with a detailed list of the legal services I could offer them. This proved very effective in getting rid of them, although sadly it never brought me any business.

Derek Wellman
Lincoln

SIR – When I receive cold calls, I turn the tables by asking them, 'And vot is your passverd?' It really throws them.

Anne Wainwright
Chalfont St Peter, Buckinghamshire

SIR – My husband's reply to yet another offer of new windows and doors: 'We are not interested; you see, we live in a tent.'

Elizabeth Waring
Hambledon, Surrey

SIR – Seven years after my husband's death, I still have cold callers asking to speak to him. I suggest they pop down to the cemetery, where they are sure to find him as he doesn't get out much.

Shirley Banks
Bradley, North Yorkshire

YOUR CALL IS NOT IMPORTANT TO US

SIR – I recently telephoned my car insurers to discuss the rather large increase in my renewal premium. When I was put on hold for some time the background music was a rendition of 'We have all the time in the world'. I didn't. I hung up.

Elaine Winter
Whyteleafe, Surrey

SIR – During the 95 minutes that I was being assured by HMRC that 'one of our advisers will be with you as soon as possible', I managed to do my internet grocery shop, cook the children's tea, prepare their next day's packed lunches, empty the dishwasher, bring in the washing, feed the chickens and clear the table.

At the 96th minute, I was unceremoniously cut off.

Dial six if you are losing the will to live.

Rachel Collins
Otterbourne, Hampshire

SIR – BT Infinity broadband: you think it's about speed, but it's actually about time.

Alex Perry
Thames Ditton, Surrey

DOMESTIC CONUNDRUMS

SIR – Why, whenever I put a cup of liquid in my microwave, does the wretched machine always come to rest with the handle facing away from me?

David Hughes
South Wonston, Hampshire

SIR – Why do pill manufacturers provide packs of six for those of us who live with seven-day weeks?

Paul Wigmore
Bitton, Gloucestershire

SIR – I read that a couple who have already adopted five disabled children have been refused a sixth because the flex on their kettle is deemed too long and therefore a health and safety risk.

Perhaps it could be shortened and the surplus used to throttle the person who made this decision.

Leonard Glynn
Bristol

SIR — With all due respect to the physicists looking for the God particle, perhaps they should be looking at a more fundamental problem: why do Christmas lights never work when they are unpacked, yet they worked perfectly when they were put away?

P. Hull
Hoo, Kent

THE DAY OF DRINK

SIR — If church services were not so goddamned boring, the clergy would have nothing to fear from extended Sunday opening.

Then again, the nonsense spouted by most clerics, from the inept and now departing Archbishop of Canterbury downwards, is enough to drive a man to drink, rather than to Oxford Street.

Robert Warner
West Woodhay, Berkshire

SIR — While wishing the Archbishop of Canterbury a long and peaceful retirement, I do hope he will now be able to find time to have a proper haircut, a decent shave and an eyebrow trim.

Frances Speakman
Cranbrook, Essex

SINKING SARTORIAL STANDARDS

SIR – I am constantly appalled by the decline in dress in this country. In the evening, when I sit in the bar of my local restaurant, I am treated to a procession of people of all ages wearing anoraks, tracksuits and trainers. Women with bottoms the size of the *Titanic* appear in tights, and well-bellied middle-aged men walk in with their shirts untucked.

Go to any other European country to see how smartly people dress when they go out. Have we lost our personal and national pride?

A 93-year-old friend walked into a shop last week and asked to see a sports jacket. The assistant said, 'What have you got in mind, mate? Adidas or Nike?'

I rest my case.

Graham Masterton
Tadworth Park, Surrey

SIR – I deplore the rise of the rucksack. A gentleman should have a leather briefcase and a lady a handbag.

Ted Shorter
Hildenborough, Kent

SIR – You quote a police constable calling some of the women at Ladies' Day at Aintree 'Tramps'. I disagree with him; I would have used the word 'Trollops'.

Roger Marsh
Morecambe, Lancashire

SIR – With regards to the Epsom Derby, when did it become de rigueur to wear wrap-around sun glasses with a black silk top hat?

Deirdre Lay
Peaslake, Surrey

SIR – I am always charmed when a passing stranger tips his hat. Am I right in supposing this practice is now confined to gentlemen over the age of 70?

Caroline Birch
Boldre, Hampshire

SIR – Are my wife and I the only two people left who manage to wear a warm scarf without putting the two ends through a loop?

Peter J. Smith
Shirley, Surrey

SIR – Your correspondent's dilemma over choosing between expensive outerwear and underwear is not new. I remember my mother describing certain women as 'all fur coat and no knickers'.

James Hewitt
Lowdham, Nottinghamshire

SIR – Your correspondent with no pockets should keep her mobile phone in her bra, as does a friend of mine. I'm told it is quite pleasant to receive a call.

C.J.W.
Warlingham, Surrey

SIR – Can I ask when women's shoes are going to become attractive again? Wedges and one-inch soles are simply ugly. The fair sex dress to please us (I think), but this man isn't pleased.

Anthony Messenger
Windsor, Berkshire

SIR – My father, who is nearly 84, is occasionally seen at breakfast sporting a sarong, a form of dress picked up from his military service in Malaya.

Elaine Higgins
Colchester, Essex

SIR – It has long been a tradition in our family that the main use of the flannel is to protect one's modesty in case anyone comes into the bathroom by mistake.

Tim Wilson
Bradfield, Berkshire

SIR – I was recently contemplating the person who won the £60 million lottery and wondered what I would do in such a position. I concluded I would give most of it away, but my one luxury indulgence would be a brand new pair of socks every day. Heaven.

Richard Walford
Knowle, Devon

TIES THAT BLIND

SIR – As an octogenarian I wear a tie whenever I am out. As proof of this I have a photo of myself taken on a beach in the 1930s wearing a bathing costume complete with a shirt and tie.

Greg Hayward
Corfe Mullen, Dorset

SIR – I'm not too sure how many ties I've got; I only know I have enough to hold my trousers up for the rest of my life.

Bob Addison
Hartlepool

SIR – I wore a tie virtually every day in my career. I shall not throw any away as they may prove useful as napkins or bibs as I grow older.

Robert Kemp
Goonhavern, Cornwall

SIR – My ties always have a great time whenever I visit a lap dancing club.

Clive Pilley
Westcliff-on-Sea, Essex

SIR – I once had a tie embroidered with hedgehogs. When asked, I would explain that it was a constant reminder that we are surrounded by pricks.

Robert Whittle
Hook, Hampshire

PAST MY SELL-BY DATE

SIR – I realised I was past my sell-by date when, reaching the supermarket checkout, I was asked, 'Would you like help with packing?' I had only one item of shopping in my basket. Is it time to check out?

Ann Lill
Kingston, East Sussex

SIR – Vis-à-vis the news on the radio this morning that wolf whistling may be an offence, I recently received several wolf whistles as I passed a building site, teetering on my high heels. Instead of feeling demeaned I was very grateful, in view of my advancing years. I thanked the offending perpetrators, much to their astonishment, and went on my way with a lighter step.

Ingrid Brewer
Bristol

SIR – I was surprised to find that my improved level of contentment now that I approach old age is due to my 'better coping ability' and 'lowering of expectations'.

And there was me thinking it was due to the children having finally flown the nest and the mortgage being fully paid off.

Peter Fayers
Coulsdon, Surrey

SIR – You report that weightlifting and aerobics may help slow down memory problems. I guess the first problem is remembering where you left the weights.

D.P. Laycock
Castlemorton, Worcestershire

SIR – There might be a positive side to email snooping. When I inadvertently delete a vital email, text or folder, as I so often do, will a quick call to a bright young thing at GCHQ resolve my problem?

Heather M. Tanner
Earl Soham, Suffolk

SIR – A 70-year life should more than adequately prepare us for eternity, wherever spent. Indeed, I find that one summer of BBC repeats, coupled with six-hour sessions of golf, tennis, Formula I and bowls, is doing the trick nicely.

Robert Stephenson
Henley-on-Thames, Oxfordshire

SIR – Even in my depths of disease and sometimes despair, standing up from my bed for examination by a young lady doctor I could not help but retort, 'I beg your pardon?' when she asked, 'Look right, look left, now up, and then down to the non-chest area.'

Yo, ho, ho.

Michael Peckitt
Cheltenham, Gloucestershire

SIR — You report that a 78-year-old grandfather-of-four is to have a sex change operation on the NHS. At the tender age of 65, I was recently knocked back by my NHS dentist when I asked about having a couple of dental implants.

Perhaps I, too, should opt for a sex change operation and try to persuade the NHS to do my teeth while they're at it.

James L. Shearer
Edinburgh

SIR — I visited my dentist yesterday. In addition to warning me of the risks of oral cancer related to alcohol, as in your report, he warned me that the other major risk factors were smoking (anything) and oral sex. I feel there is a moral to be drawn from this, but I am not sure what it is.

Kenneth Hynes
London N7

HEROIC SMOKERS

SIR – Smokers should be treated as heroes, not pariahs. They should be given a medal, cosseted and encouraged. Consider: when I gave up, cigarettes were 45p for twenty; the last time I looked it was nearly £5. Nearly all of this is tax.

These selfless individuals are, at their own expense, voluntarily funding large parts of government expenditure. Much of the aforesaid applies to drinkers, too.

Nicholas Wightwick
Rossett, Cheshire

SIR – It's good to hear that cigarettes might be sold in plain packets; there will be much more room for Government policy to be worked out.

Malcolm Parkin
Kinnesswood, Kinross-shire

A YEAR IN POLITICS

HOW TO SPOT A BAD
PRIME MINISTER

SIR — I have just realised the solution to our
economic and political problems: we must never
again allow anyone with a five-letter surname to
become prime minister. The four most recent
examples surely prove my point.

Stephen Malyon
Paignton, Devon

SIR — Tony Blair's recent comment, 'I have learned
an immense amount in the past five years' appears to
contain one 'l' too many.

David Law
Salisbury

SIR — It is an interesting anomaly that however
wealthy the Blair family becomes, the only word
which always describes them most appropriately is
'cheap'.

Mick Ferrie
Mawnan Smith, Cornwall

SIR – I read that Gordon Brown has been appointed United Nations Special Envoy for Global Education. Can this be the same Gordon Brown who spoke of 'one pence' in a budget speech as Chancellor?

Geoffrey Hodgson
Shadwell, West Yorkshire

SIR – Has Gordon Brown been running Rangers FC since he ceased to be Prime Minister?

Jon Redfern
Cleobury Mortimer, Shropshire

SIR – The present Government has been in power for the best part of two years, but *The Daily Telegraph* is still publishing letters criticising Gordon Brown. Surely it is time for you and your readers to move on and start complaining about the poor job that David Cameron and his clowns are doing?

Clive Pilley
Westcliff-on-Sea, Essex

A COALITION OF CLOWNS

SIR – I have never found a collective noun for clowns. If there isn't one, may I humbly suggest a *coalition*.

Peter Pascall
Worsley, Lancashire

SIR – So the Queen has endured 12 of them. How about *a plague* of prime ministers?

John Bridge
Mannings Heath, West Sussex

SIR – So Nick Clegg wants to be a novelist? Then I hope he takes this advice: 'Go! Wait no longer, lest the Muse leave thee! Get thee to a garret and write!'

Ginny Martin
Bishop's Waltham, Hampshire

SIR – Come back, John Prescott. All is forgiven.

Bruce Chalmers
Goring-by-Sea, West Sussex

SIR – Is it not odd, and a trifle spooky, that the two Tory ministers whom Labour have gone after are Fox and Hunt? What can it mean?

Nicholas Guitard
Poundstock, Cornwall

SIR – Perhaps Louise Mensch would be taken more seriously if she didn't use phrases such as 'sitting down with my whip' – unless she said it on purpose.

Geoff Wright
Doncaster, South Yorkshire

SIR – Before we have a Cabinet reshuffle, could we have a new dealer, please?

Frank McGarry
Lyme Regis, Dorset

SIR – It is claimed that a country gets the politicians it deserves. I'm struggling to identify just what it is we have done to be so undeserving.

Michael Hinchliffe
Smeeth, Kent

SIR – The flaw in modern democracy is that we only get to vote for those who put themselves up for election.

Anne Carter
Llanddewi, Powys

CHILLAXING WITH DAVE

SIR – I note that David Cameron is 'chillaxing'. Does the presence of this monstrous word on the front page of *The Daily Telegraph* mean that it has now moved to common use? Or is there a subliminal message that Mr Cameron is turning into a chilling axe man, as many would have us believe?

Stuart Taylor
Oxford

SIR – I do think your correspondent is being more than generous when he refers to Mr Cameron as a halfwit.

Steve Revill
Nottingham

SIR – I will risk becoming unpopular, says David Cameron. When, might I ask, did he imagine he was anything but?

G.P.
Chester

SIR – Fresh-faced, rosy-cheeked, inexperienced schoolboys having frivolous adventures are fine in the novels of *Just William* or *Jennings*. But running the country is no place for them. As a lifelong Conservative, I am finding the Cameron Gang a tad disappointing.

David Tucker
High Wycombe, Buckinghamshire

SIR – The caption to your photograph suggests that the Prime Minister had found a few spare coins to support a young busker playing the French horn. Can we be sure that he wasn't helping himself to the takings?

Gareth Williams
Berkeley, Gloucestershire

SIR – If I give a fiver to the Conservatives will they guarantee that I will never, ever, have to meet David Cameron?

Ron Matthews
La Brévière, Normandy, France

SIR – With all this well-documented jogging, why isn't David Cameron getting thinner?

Hubert van den Bergh
London SW1

SIR – Would it not be wonderful if we could alter the rules a bit and have Aung San Suu Kyi as Prime Minister?

Alexander Tulloch
Folkestone, Kent

SIR – I wonder, does David Cameron read the papers?

Richard Davies
Heath Charnock, Lancashire

SIR – I feel that David Cameron has chosen the wrong job. With so many of his friends, Cabinet members, press secretaries and old school chums facing prosecution, he should have been a lawyer and helped them in their time of need.

Derek Hanlin
Gilfach Goch, Rhondda

THE REAL LEVESON IN QUIRY

SIR – I wonder if the good Lord Leveson would mind taking a short break from his exacting task to make a judicial statement about the correct pronunciation of his name. Opinion seems to be divided pretty well 50/50 as to whether the *eve* bit is as in 'Adam and Eve' or as in 'heavenly'.

The suspense of waiting to hear which option the next speaker will select is beginning to get on my wick.

Margaret Kimberley
West Mersea, Essex

SIR – No doubt many people at Westminster are now trying to decide if LOL means 'lots of lies' or 'look out – Leveson'.

Angus Robertson
Durness-by-Lairg, Sutherland

SIR – I'm baffled: how do Cabinet Ministers have the time to send so many texts and emails? Do they dictate them to a civil servant? Or do they use predictive text or shorthand, such as 'gr8 news Rup'?

Ian Henderson
Witney, Oxfordshire

SIR – Having watched Jeremy Paxman's appearance before the Leveson Inquiry, I was struck by the poor quality of the inquisition from Robert Jay QC. Perhaps it would have been better to pay Paxman to run the inquiry. He would probably be cheaper, too.

Tony Graham
Loch Awe, Argyll

SIR – I am surprised that witnesses have not refused to answer any questions until such time as Robert Jay QC shaves off his ghastly facial growth.

Nicky Samengo-Turner
Hundon, Suffolk

SIR – What do the legions of no doubt highly paid ladies and gentlemen sitting in the background at the Leveson Inquiry do all day? One rotund chap has spent several months picking his nose. I wrote to the Inquiry officials for clarification but received no enlightenment. I wonder if there are any vacancies.

G.M.
London SW17

SIR – I hope the Leveson Inquiry ends soon; I've had more than enough of photos of Jeremy Hunt and his bicycle.

Edward Huxley
Thorpe, Surrey

SIR – So James Naughtie's slip of the tongue was right after all.

Roger Smith
Meppershall, Bedfordshire

THE SUN OF GOD

SIR – Why criticise John Sentamu for writing a column in the new *Sun on Sunday*? Jesus would have done the same.

Gail Coates
Trowbridge, Wiltshire

SIR – As an incurably forgetful person with no experience of running a multinational corporation, I feel I am more than qualified to replace James Murdoch. In fact, I already have no recollection of submitting my application later today.

Dominic Pike
Edinburgh

SIR – At last it has emerged that 'Mr Cameron probably rode the horse more than Mrs Brooks'. One is bound to ask, therefore: how often did he ride Mrs Brooks?

David Townson
Isleworth, Middlesex

KEN'S SPIN CYCLES

SIR – If Boris loses the London mayoral election, what are we going to call the bikes?

Ian Cannons
Bradfield, Essex

SIR – I have just heard Ken Livingstone claiming on LBC Radio that it was his entrepreneurial spirit that led him to set up a company to avoid paying full income tax. If Mr Livingstone is an entrepreneur then I'm a ballerina.

Bob Stebbings
Chorleywood, Hertfordshire

SIR – I do find it funny that people seem to envisage their taxes being spent on the police or the NHS. I always see mine spent on a departmental bonding game of paintball, followed by slap-up pizzas all round.

Chris Thorpe
Tonbridge, Kent

SIR – I have been helping Jimmy Carr reduce his tax bill for many years by avoiding his products.

Michael Carrington
Wilby, Northamptonshire

SIR – Wouldn't it be much more interesting if David Cameron and George Osborne came clean about their antics when members of the Bullingdon Club, instead of boring us with their tax returns?

William Rusbridge
Tregony, Cornwall

THE POSH PARTY

SIR – The Leader of the House of Lords, Thomas Galloway Dunlop du Roy de Blicquy Galbraith, 2nd Baron Strathclyde, claims that the Conservatives are not the rich, posh party.

Indeed, how would he know?

Jack Woodford
Buckfastleigh, Devon

SIR – There can be no better example of how out of touch this Government is than George Osborne's constant use of the dropped 't' and the glottal stop – a wholly unconvincing attempt to ingratiate himself with the masses. In this mixed, but essentially Conservative, part of East Kent, I have never heard anyone speak as he does.

Elizabeth Weston
Sandwich, Kent

SIR – Never mind the price of milk, have the posh boys ever stood in a queue at Heathrow for two hours?

M.F.
Berkhamsted, Hertfordshire

SIR – What is wrong with being posh?

Alan Sabatini
Bournemouth

SIR – If Ed Miliband refers to David Cameron and his Cabinet as 'posh boys', is it politically correct to refer to Mr Miliband and his gang as 'plebs'?

Craig Kennedy
Brookfield, Renfrewshire

AUSTERITY BRITAIN IN THE SOUP

SIR – My wife says there was a recipe for bread soup in your *Weekend* section. I knew the economy wasn't in the best shape, but it's not that bad, surely?

T.H.
Hawkinge, Kent

SIR – You report that arrests have been made in connection with the discovery of 4 million counterfeit pound coins. Far from being charged, surely these enterprising individuals should be rewarded for their entrepreneurial flair? After all, they are only assisting the Bank of England with its programme of quantitative easing, while relieving the taxpayer of the minting costs.

Alan Duncalf
Bampton, Devon

SIR – Walking through the ancient streets of Shrewsbury last night I was assailed by one of the many people apparently down on his luck and begging for money. I decided to ignore him as he was making a call on his pristine iPhone 4.

John D. Neal
Shrewsbury

SIR – The world economy is like a game of Monopoly. The Chinese, Indians and Arabs have got all the money and the best property; we've got the Old Kent Road.

P.J. Minns
Frilford, Oxfordshire

SIR – May I suggest that Sodom in North Wales and Upham in Hampshire be introduced to each other as a well-suited twinning partnership in the present political climate.

Roy Thomas
Walmley, West Midlands

GRANNY ATTACKS

SIR – Surely the so-called granny tax is merely a convoluted way of withdrawing the winter fuel allowance?

Barbara Dewick
Bookham, Surrey

SIR – Why don't we old folk just belt up and try to help? We have had it so good. Many of us could well afford to buy our daily aspirin from the chemist, pay for our own Viagra and send back the winter heating allowance in order to support those in real need.

Come on, guys, we know who we are.

Christopher Richardson
London N7

SIR – Today is my 80th birthday, and I understand that that nice Mr Osborne is marking this milestone by giving me an extra 25 pence every week to top up my state pension. Just think: next week I shall be able to afford a stamp, with which to post him a letter of thanks.

Bryan Lillywhite
Mollington, Oxfordshire

SIR – David Cameron wants to help us old people to downsize. I am already two inches shorter than I used to be, so I don't need his help.

John de Lange
London N12

SIR – Will the next suggestion from David Cameron's advisers be an annual cull of the elderly?

Gordon and Patricia James
Spalding, Lincolnshire

SIR – The call for the elderly to go back to work has forced me to consider my workplace options. Too fragile for manual labour and totally out of touch with modern office technology, what has an old codger got to offer?

Then I realised that my ability to write senseless drivel would ensure a well-paid position in Downing Street as a senior aide. Also, as downsizing would mean living in a tent, I could take up residence close to St Paul's and walk to work in the morning.

George Wilkie
Hemingford Grey, Cambridgeshire

SIR – I suppose we could all go and do the cleaning for Samantha Cameron's pals.

Les Sharp
Hersham, Surrey

SIR – Why not let the elderly run the country instead of the current bunch and solve two problems at one stroke?

Priscilla Thomas
Rode, Somerset

SIR – We are comfortably retired here on the east coast of Yorkshire, both in our seventies and reasonably fit. On reading your front page today my wife quietly but firmly exclaimed, 'We may have downsized, but I'm not going back to f****** work.'

Thomas Robertson
Bridlington, East Yorkshire

SHREDDING THE BANKERS

SIR – To satisfy everyone, could not Stephen Hester donate his bonus to the Conservatives and be awarded a knighthood – with Labour promising to remove it?

Dr John Doherty
Stratford-upon-Avon, Warwickshire

SIR – As far as I am concerned, Mr Hester may have his bonus and Mr Goodwin his knighthood in exchange for the removal of the RBS Group logo from the centre of the pitches on which Six Nations games are played.

John Carter
Bromley, Kent

SIR – My wife and I, though impoverished, would be quite happy for Mr Hester to keep his bonus, provided that he coughed up £1,000 to buy himself a decent pair of hunting boots. His present cheapos are a sartorial and sporting disgrace.

Roland Fernsby
Furneux Pelham, Hertfordshire

SIR – If the get-rich-quick riff-raff are encouraged to go into banking this is what you must expect. Banking used to be an honourable profession.

Duncan Rayner
Sunningdale, Berkshire

SIR – The rationale for the high salaries of bankers has been that it is necessary to obtain people of the right calibre. I would prefer people of a different calibre.

Mik Shaw
Goring-by-Sea, West Sussex

SIR – Is a British banker's word now his subprime bond?

David Pitts
East Molesey, Surrey

SIR – Now that Fred Goodwin has been stripped of his knighthood, what steps can be taken to change his surname, so that people of unsullied reputation are no longer damned by association?

Gareth D.J. Goodwin
Wrington, Somerset

SIR – Mr Goodwin should have been given an asterisk instead, so that anyone writing about Sir* Fred would have to add an explanatory footnote.

Keith Macpherson
Houston, Renfrewshire

SIR – Perhaps Mr Goodwin should change his first name to 'Sir Fred' and raise the proverbial two fingers at the anti-business mob, including David Cameron.

Phillipa Allen
London N2

SUPER PASTY

SIR – I don't recall anyone asking whether Winston Churchill or Harold Macmillan ate pasties – hot or otherwise.

R.Q.
West Drayton, Middlesex

SIR – Will it be necessary to re-name Hot Cross Buns 'Cold Hot Cross Buns'?

John Hodges
Woodstock, Oxfordshire

SIR – Help needed: how do I get pasties out of a Jerry Can?

B. Jefferson
Nottingham

SIR – While waiting patiently in the queue for petrol for my lawnmower, I failed to hear the order that we must now refer to Jerry Cans as Saxon Cans.

Lt Col S.M.P. Stewart (retd)
Hexham, Northumberland

SIR — What a fantastic Government we have. They manage to create a fuel shortage before a strike has even been called.

Nick Hallam
Verwood, Dorset

SIR — I am glad the weekend is over, as I was finding it difficult to separate Government policy from April Fools' jokes.

Mike Gidley
Faversham, Kent

SIR — As a matter of passing interest, is the Labour Party in dormant mode, or is it deliberately keeping a low profile as a cunning ploy while the Government lurches nonchalantly from one crisis to another?

Gavin Littaur
London NW4

MILIBAND THE YOUNGER

SIR — Am I alone in being unable to listen to Ed Miliband without being struck by his remarkable similarity to that other great politician, William Pitt the Younger — as played in the comedy series *Blackadder*.

Dominic Regan
Little Coxwell, Oxfordshire

SIR – Am I alone in thinking that Ed Miliband comes across as a truculent school prefect who has again failed in his desire to become Head Boy?

Ian Currie
Winchester, Hampshire

SIR – Ed Miliband must stop starting his interview replies with, 'I guess what I'm saying is . . .' If he has to guess at what his own ideas are, what hope has he of understanding anyone else's?

Rev. Philip Foster
Hemingford Abbots, Cambridgeshire

SIR – Your columnist Mary Riddell usually makes me so angry that internal bleeding occurs with no need for any help from the aspirin I take. But today she made me laugh out loud twice: once by comparing Mr Miliband to Clement Attlee; the second time by stating that the Labour Party needs Ed Balls to fight and win an election.

How I roared!

S.P.
Headcorn, Kent

GALLOWAY: CAD OR BOUNDER?

SIR – If George Galloway can win an amazing by-election, with his opponent attributing his victory to his appearance on *Big Brother*, does this indicate a way forward for David Miliband?

Ken Wortelhock
Orewa Beach, New Zealand

SIR – In asking whether George Galloway is a cad or a bounder your correspondent does not say what the difference is. I was once told that a bounder is a young subaltern who, on being told by his colonel to break the news to a brother officer's wife that her husband has been taken prisoner, consoles her so successfully that he ends up making love to her; whereas a cad, on being given the same task, has a bath and shave in order to increase his chances of achieving the same result.

Readers will make up their own minds whether either of these descriptions fits Mr Galloway.

Gareth Howlett
Edinburgh

SIR – Whatever one's view of George Galloway, one must admire his indefatigability.

Gordon Galletly
Halstead, Kent

SIR – Having been dead set against independence for Scotland, I have recently changed my mind. It may cost the rest of the United Kingdom a few billion but it would open up the possibility of being able to deport George Galloway as an undesirable alien.

M.B.
Overton-on-Dee, Wrexham

LITTLER BRITAIN

SIR – Just a thought: if Scotland does achieve full independence, what will be left? Little Britain?

John Thorndycraft
Greenford, Middlesex

SIR – If Scotland votes for independence, presumably the cost of a stamp will be drastically reduced?

M.O'C.
Sarratt, Hertfordshire

SIR – If Scotland secedes from the UK our grandchildren will become foreigners. Should my wife and I be allowed some say in the matter?

Graham Creedy
Uffington, Lincolnshire

SIR – If the Union Flag is redesigned, can we please have something that looks the same no matter which way up it is flown?

Tom Swift
Fareham, Hampshire

SIR – How long after independence would Scotland follow Rangers FC into administration?

Eldon Sandys
Pyrford, Surrey

SIR – If independence means less of Alex Salmond on our radio and television, bring it on.

Michael H. Peters
Sittingbourne, Kent

SIR – Alex Salmond, Nicola Sturgeon? Something sounds a bit fishy to me.

Joan Campanini
Twickenham, Middlesex

SIR – After many years, our close friendship with a professional Scottish couple came under serious review when they invited my wife and me to a supper of haggis with boiled turnips. Until this incident, we had regarded them as quite cultured.

Raymond Barry
Laytham, East Yorkshire

THE HOUSE OF BARS

SIR – What most disappointed and outraged me, upon learning of Eric Joyce's brawl in a House of Commons bar, was that it was not shown on the otherwise dreary and tiresome Parliamentary channel.

Nicky Samengo-Turner
Hundon, Suffolk

SIR – Am I alone in my admiration for Keith Davies, the Welsh Assembly member who has been criticised for a noisy drinking binge at a Cardiff hotel? In the first place, he was in full cry at 4.45 a.m., when almost all lesser mortals were long abed. In the second place, the woman with him was not his wife. And thirdly, most impressively, the man is 71 years old. The criticism must be inspired by envy.

D.McC.
London W14

SIR – I never usually have reason to doubt the accuracy of Ian Cowie's financial column. However, I was most upset to see an accompanying picture of a belly dancer to illustrate his reference to a striptease. As a former belly dancer, it brought on a shimmy of rage. We remain clothed at all times – a fact which, I am sure, certain MPs might sorrowfully confirm to you.

Mrs Brenda Love
Wimborne, Dorset

PRESCOTT'S PENSION

SIR – Am I alone in thinking that Lord Prescott has been all over the airwaves like a rash of late? I thought the main purpose of pensioning off second-rate political hacks to the House of Lords was to get them out of our hair.

Simon Allen
Colemans Hatch, East Sussex

SIR – John Prescott has scored a blinder with the compensation for intrusion into his phone calls. Anyone hacking his account would need at least a degree in Double Dutch to be able to decipher a single word. Even Bletchley Park would have been stumped.

Frank Hall
Ramsgate, Kent

SILLY BERCOW

SIR — Sally (or should that be Silly?) Bercow is at it again. In a message to the 45,000 sad sacks who lead such dull lives that they have nothing better to do than follow the stupid antics of this woman on Twitter, she tweeted that she is tempted to try the latest legal high.

Can no one shut her up?

Robert Readman
Bournemouth, Dorset

SIR — Tom Stoppard does not Twitter. I do not Twitter. Extracts from Twitter show clearly that those who do are bird-brained.

Brian Coomber
Shoreham-by-Sea, West Sussex

SIR — John Bercow's delivery of his 'kaleidoscope' speech in front of the Queen was worthy of Jane Austen's Mr Collins. Should the BBC ever be tempted to commission another adaptation of *Pride and Prejudice*, that's one piece of casting taken care of.

Mark Shirley
London SW6

SIR — Strange how the nation's First Commoner, Mr Bercow, can deport himself in full regalia when appearing at Westminster Hall, but presents himself like a prep-school master when doing his most important job, presiding over the House of Commons. Can we have a return to the proper robes of office in the near future?

P.H.
Kingsbridge, Devon

WE'VE NEVER HAD IT
SO SHABBILY

SIR – In today's paper there was a photo of the Prime Minister on a night off, visiting a restaurant in a navy anorak and jeans. Could you imagine Harold Macmillan ever appearing on the streets of the capital dressed in this shabby way?

I will not vote for him again.

Barry Carroll
London SW4

SIR – It is not only the Prime Minister's children who get left behind in pubs; husbands have the habit of wandering off, too. I've lost my husband on numerous occasions during the past 38 years, the most memorable being the Silver Jubilee celebrations when he fainted in the ladies' lavatory at a village garden party and turned up several hours later having been rescued by our glamorous hostess (at least that's the story he told me at the time).

On another occasion he inadvertently joined a two-hour private French tour of the roof of Reims cathedral, ending up behind a locked door and making us late for our ferry home. He was as white as a sheet due to his fear of heights.

Needless to say, I made very little effort to find him during his missing hours, enjoying what little freedom I could.

Judy Parsley
London W4

SIR – Why do our politicians feel the need to hold the hand of their spouse when attending state occasions? It is completely inappropriate. Why can't they follow the example of the Royal Family?

June Boyd
Carlisle

SIR – What is the explanation for the five cuff buttons on the suits worn by Mr Cameron and Mr Clegg? I assume neither served in a Guards regiment.

T.M. Trelawny Gower
Lowestoft, Suffolk

THE ARMY'S WARS

SIR – Your headline screams, 'Army wages war over battalion cuts'. The way things are going for the Services, it may well soon be the only war it can wage.

Lt Col Charles Holden (retd)
Lymington, Hampshire

SIR – I am delighted to hear naval personnel are getting a new uniform. Now all we need are some ships to put them in.

Major Nigel Price
Marple Bridge, Cheshire

SIR – There has been great activity in the skies above our house today. Are both the planes in the Royal Air Force in action?

Sarah Castley
Peterborough, Cambridgeshire

SIR – I am often asked why we need our Armed Forces. What, they ask, is the threat?

My response is always the same: the threat is the Treasury.

Group Captain David Greenway (retd)
Andover, Hampshire

SIR – Ah well, when the Army vanishes we can always send in Prince Harry, the dancing Prince, in his blue desert boots. He'll disarm anyone with murderous intent with his charming smile.

Elizabeth Davies
Papworth Everard, Cambridgeshire

KINGS, QUEENS
AND JOKERS

THE STUDENTS' PRINCESS

SIR — My housemates and I are students at Newcastle University. We recently decided that whenever you print a photograph of Kate Middleton on the front page of your paper, one of us has to buy it, cut it out and stick it on our fridge. I don't know what this says about us, especially as the boys down the road at the local polytechnic do something quite similar, just with Page Three glamour models from their lads' mags.

Edward Bunn
Newcastle University

SIR — Why do newspapers dissect everything the Duchess of Cambridge wears to official engagements? I am sure I wouldn't appreciate my local paper reporting along similar lines:

'Mrs Howes had lunch at the Castle Hotel today, wearing a dress from Phase Eight costing £100, together with a tatty T-shirt picked up for £2 in Porto market last year.'

Kerrie Howes
Llangorse, Powys

SIR – The Duchess, you report, 'wore a full-length dress by Alice Temperley'. Once again I am left wondering who designed the Duke's suit, tie, socks and shoes. When will the editor stop teasing us in this way?

Yours in anticipation,

J.J. Forshaw
Ormskirk, Lancashire

SIR – To relieve the monotony of carrying pictures of the Middleton females almost daily on your front page, may I suggest that a snatched photograph of the family's tom-cat at play in their garden would be a welcome change?

Derrick Collier
Wroxton, Oxfordshire

SIR – Why does your newspaper make such a fuss about Pippa Middleton? I see better-looking girls in the queue for Greggs in Walsall.

Kevin Platt
Walsall, West Midlands

SIR – If Pippa Middleton became a celebrity for her derrière, why are we constantly bombarded with her non-newsworthy frontage?

Yvonne de Mellow
Rowlands Castle, Hampshire

SIR – I think the readers have the right to know whether she is, in fact, the editor's secret love child.

> **G.S.**
> Writtle, Essex

UPPITY MIDDLETONS

SIR – Are there now four classes in this country: Working, Middle, Middleton and Upper?

> **A.J.**
> Stoke Gabriel, Devon

SIR – Call me an old-fashioned left-footer, but I couldn't help being shocked to see the number of people chewing gum at a Church of England confirmation service recently. One of them even complained to me that she'd had trouble pushing her gum to one side when she took communion.

I learned at the party afterwards that these people or their spouses worked in so-called professions. Why do they think it's acceptable to chew in front of the Bishop or, for that matter, before their Maker? Is this another Middleton effect?

> **Gabriel Herbert**
> London W12

PINS-IN-WAITING

SIR – I don't know whether the Queen keeps a £5 note in her handbag, as you report, but I can confirm, with some relief, that at least one of her late ladies-in-waiting used to keep safety pins in hers.

On duty once, I became painfully conscious that the straps holding up an ancient kilt were beginning to disintegrate. Fearing a disaster, I moved close to the lady-in-waiting and inquired if she happened to be carrying any safety pins. Not only did she confirm she was, she whispered, 'Don't worry, I will keep an eye on you and if I see you behaving as if you have a ruptured hernia, I will come to your rescue.'

Iain Thornber
Morvern, Argyllshire

PRINCE OF OXFAM

SIR – Support for the monarchy would be even greater were Prince Charles to give his brown overcoat and double-breasted suit to Oxfam (assuming they would take them), and if Princess Anne were to stop imitating the late Kim Jong-il's hair style.

Barry Thomas
Bury St Edmunds, Suffolk

SIR — Yesterday we saw Prince Charles posing a foot off the ground, looking like a starched monkey on a wall. Today he is seen 'joining in' the games at a youth rally, wearing a morning suit, tie, cufflinks, a formal handkerchief and what, appallingly, appear to be trousers with a crease. Why is there no appropriate royal dress for such informal occasions?

Geoff Milburn
Glossop, Derbyshire

SIR — Today was the final straw. I am a great fan of the Royal Family, but I get very upset when Prince Charles is repeatedly shown with his hands in his pockets (see the picture on page eight of him buying a doughnut).

Had he served in the Army, his Sergeant Major would have him repeatedly on fatigues with no royal excuses. Please, Charles, if your hands are cold, wear gloves.

Lt Col T.W.P. Overton (retd)
Goodworth Clatford, Hampshire

SIR – Please don't judge the younger royals too harshly for walking with their hands in their pockets; they obviously haven't been brought up properly. The television pictures showed the Duke of Edinburgh displaying the same slovenly habit on his walkabout after church last Sunday.

Jonathan L. Kelly
Yatton, North Somerset

SIR – Given that the Queen is now referred to as 'The Diamond Queen', it would be most appropriate for the Duke of Edinburgh to be known as 'The Diamond Geezer'.

Howard Spivey
Preston, Gloucestershire

SIR – With regards to the body found on the Queen's Sandringham Estate, has anyone heard from Fergie recently?

Robert Readman
Bournemouth, Dorset

ONE IS NOT ENTERTAINED

SIR – Having watched some of the Jubilee Concert,
I do hope someone had the consideration to provide
Queen Victoria with earplugs.

David R. Boswell
Timsbury, Somerset

SIR – Having been around for the original
Coronation, I had no intention of watching a
concert by 'pop' artists for the Jubilee. I then took
a glass of wine to my wife, who was watching the
television, and for some reason I started to watch
what I can only describe as the most enjoyable show I
have seen for quite some time.

The small bottle of wine was replaced, and
we continued to dance away the evening in a
modernistic style. What a wonderful way to show the
world that the British are the masters at putting on
the style.

Now, can any of your readers help in erasing the
'Ob-La-Di, Ob-La-Da' song from our heads?

Alan Cubbin
Tunstall, North Yorkshire

LET THEM WATCH CAKE

SIR – As I write this, the BBC is choosing to celebrate the reigning monarch's procession along the Thames with a televised discussion about cake.

Stuart Rose
Wilcott, Shropshire

SIR – I believe there was a magnificent river pageant on the Thames on Sunday. Sadly, I missed most of it; I was watching BBC One.

P.L.
Preston, Lancashire

SIR – Did the BBC select John Barrowman to present live coverage from the Belfry Barge in the mistaken belief that 'campanology' meant something entirely different?

Andrew Holmes
Bromley, Kent

SIR – For me the BBC excels in the Banal, the Biased and the Common.

Lesley Benson
Ipswich, Suffolk

SIR – The next sixty years will be even better if we can dispense with the BBC and the *Guardian*.

Mary Lloyd-Jones
Guildford, Surrey

SIR – A BBC commentator kept stating that HMS *Belfast* displaced 91,000 tons when almost any fool would know that it was more likely to be 9,000 tons; he also kept referring to the British Navy rather than the Royal Navy.

However, my biggest irritation was the fact that a civilian on the Royal barge, who clearly had an important role to play, was wearing brown shoes with a blue suit.

David Miller
Maidenhead, Berkshire

SIR – I heard the RCM Chamber Choir described as 'mildly eccentric'. Mildly eccentric? Absolutely barking, I say, and thank God. This is what has made this country what it is and why we continue to live here, despite the politicians.

Andrew Harvey
Zelah, Cornwall

SIR – How is it that when even local BBC television producers can make a small puddle in a supermarket car park look like a large and dramatic flood, their whole organisation managed to make last Sunday's event on the Thames so boring?

Michael Cooper
Ashcott, Somerset

SIR – Am I alone in thinking that the debate about the BBC's coverage of the Jubilee river pageant has been rather more engaging than the event itself?

Graham Mallion
Bromley, Kent

SIR – Having watched the Jubilee parade on the Thames in the rain, can we now look forward to the Winter Olympics next month?

Roy Stainton
Poole, Dorset

SPORTING TRIUMPH AND DISASTER

BRIAN MOORE PM CH OM

SIR – Having watched all the Six Nations games
in which Brian Moore has been commentating,
would it be possible to appoint him Prime Minister,
Chancellor of the Exchequer, Foreign Secretary and
Home Secretary – in fact just have him as a one-man
government – as he clearly knows everything about
everything?

Such a talent should not be wasted to the
nation.

John Mutter
Billericay, Essex

SIR – Anne Robinson once superciliously asked what
was the point of Wales. She obviously doesn't watch
rugby. Or sing.

Joyce Chadwick
Stratford-upon-Avon, Warwickshire

SIR – What has happened to 'rugger'? I have not
heard it used for years. Has it been banished by the
new professionalism of the RFU? Or was it just too
reminiscent of public-school speak?

Chris Harding
Parkstone, Dorset

THE ELITE BOAT RACE

SIR – Anyone who has slight guilt pangs about elitist tendencies can be reassured by what happened during the University Boat Race. I understand that the gentleman who disrupted the race (I will not dignify him by stating his name) was privately educated and attended one of the UK's best universities. So an elite education can develop a person into an unemployable and ignorant oaf as equally as the most disadvantaged background.

Richard Wyndham
Nacton, Suffolk

SIR – What a travesty of justice. That moronic swimmer should be flogged, keelhauled and then hanged, drawn and quartered. What a pity the umpire's launch didn't run him down.

R.J. Crawford
Blackford, Perthshire

SIR – Trenton Oldfield is such a wimp that he could not even go for a swim without a wetsuit.

Philip Roe
St Albans, Hertfordshire

SIR – The chaos surrounding the Boat Race would have been seen in the Roman Empire as a portent of chaos to come. These days, of course, we are all so rational, but I would caution the government not to be too cocky. Some degree of humility would be in order as we wait to see which regime in the Middle East collapses next; which American bank goes bankrupt before the summer; and which MP gets caught with his trousers down.

Timothy Stroud
Salisbury, Wiltshire

SIR – Despite all the drama of the Boat Race, the most interesting part of the television coverage came prior to the race itself. James May and Oz Clarke were in a brewery by the Thames tasting one of the beers. Both were wearing fluorescent yellow waistcoats, protective goggles, hard hats and inflatable life jackets. I'll have a pint of what they are having.

Malcolm Singleton
Hednesford, Staffordshire

THE 'GRAND' NATIONAL

SIR – Today an international television audience watched as British starting-line officials struggled, like Mr Bean in full comedic flow, with a piece of tatty-looking line, which was wrapped around horses and jockeys on several occasions.

Surely a more reliable system can be devised, or is this now beyond a nation which produced Newton, Brunel, Darwin and Shakespeare?

Roger Brown
Lincoln

SIR – As the death of a runner in the London Marathon is the 11th since 1981, can we assume that the do-gooders will move their attention from the Grand National to the Marathon?

Tony Herrington
Coundon, County Durham

SIR – I notice that the best runners in the London Marathon have to complete their 26 miles breathing in the fumes of several motorbike exhausts. Surely this cannot be good for them?

Peter Hayler
Edgworth, Lancashire

THE GAY GAME

SIR – The current media crusade to persuade homosexual footballers to 'come out of the closet' is, in my view, totally unnecessary. Given the way these modern footballers carry on – falling over and crying like sissies whenever they're touched by another player; the rather unsettling hugging and kissing whenever a player 'scores'; and the even more unsettling paddling of backsides whenever a player is substituted – I would estimate that the vast majority of these sportsmen are actually gay anyway.

They certainly act like it and, in many cases, look like it.

John Hiller
Euxton, Lancashire

SIR – Am I alone in noticing an increasing number of footballers being given a 'fist pump' from their nearest team mate when they've just cleared a ball for a corner or a throw-in. Isn't that what they're supposed to do? If I ever manage to secure gainful employment again, am I expected to seek out my nearest colleague on completion of a project and celebrate in a similar manner?

I've just finished this email: 'high five', letters page editor.

Yours Americanised,
Peter Morton
Crawley, West Sussex

THE UGLY GAME

SIR – Following the recent case at Westminster Magistrates' Court, I urge you now to cease all reporting of this ugly game and its disgusting 'role models'.

Andrew Dyke
London N21

SIR – Am I the only one highly entertained at the thought of John Terry using irony?

Tim Rann
Mirfield, West Yorkshire

SIR – Am I alone in observing that in our super-sensitive, cry-baby society, it is highly unlikely that we can get through a whole day of average loquacity without managing to offend someone?

Clearly to shout out at a sporting event, 'You ******* black ****' must (even if we are left by your ultra-sensitive organ to fill in the blanks) merit condign punishment (I suggest lingulectomy). However, it would seem that all politicians would do well to preface every public utterance with an introit such as: 'I wish sincerely to apologise to anyone who may be offended today by anything I may say.'

Charles Lewis
London N2

ELECTING THE ENGLAND FOOTBALL MANAGER

SIR — We live in a society where people elect their Member of Parliament and their local councillor, where members of building societies vote on management and shareholders on directors.

Yet the most important thing to most Englishmen is football. And when it comes to picking the manager, the public have no vote. This cannot be right.

Paul Brazier
Kingswood, Gloucestershire

SIR — So, Fabio Capello, an Italian, deserts a sinking ship. Anyone else have that déjà vu feeling?

David Isaacs
New Hartley, Northumberland

SIR — Such has been the media frenzy to install Harry Redknapp as the new England football manager, I imagine that had the Queen abdicated last night, 'arry would probably have been proclaimed King by now.

Jeremy Harris
Combe St Nicholas, Somerset

SIR – Harry Redknapp need not worry about not being able to operate a computer. If his dog is smart enough to have a bank account in Monaco, I am sure it can do his online banking for him.

Luke Grant
Pensax Common, Worcestershire

SIR – For me Roy Hodgson will be deemed to have been a success as the England manager if he can teach Wayne Rooney the words of the National Anthem.

Colin Bridger
Frimley, Surrey

THE TATTOOS ARE COMING HOME

SIR – We are told that Samson lost his strength when he had his hair cut. Could their shaven heads be the reason England's footballers performed so badly during Euro 2012?

Maybe Roy Hodgson should insist that they model their hairstyles on their 1966 counterparts, while also investigating whether their tattoos are sapping the ability of the muscles below them.

Brian Christley
Abergele, Conwy

SIR – In an interview before the quarter-final against Italy Ashley Cole said, 'We will die for each other.' While being sympathetic to the team for their narrow loss, I am still waiting.

John McHugh
Bridport, Dorset

SIR – Italy have just ruined their chances of a bailout.

Mike Bridgeman
Market Lavington, Wiltshire

SIR – In the whole history of human endeavour it is hard to imagine anything less worthwhile than football. It is boring, slow, eternally repetitive and what social cohesion it did provide has been destroyed by the vast amounts of money that have flooded into the game.

Therefore, to see David Cameron with his arms raised in salute of this immensely silly game makes me wonder if we have the right man for the task ahead.

Alan Pickering
Barton under Needwood, Staffordshire

SIR – The exit of England from Euro 2012 has been timed perfectly; the nation may now move on to the exit of Andy Murray from Wimbledon.

I was getting concerned that the two might overlap.

Brian Lait
Larnaca, Cyprus

LOW-FLYING MURRAYS

SIR – I switched on Radio 4 this morning to be greeted with what sounded like the drone of a low-flying light aircraft. After a minute or so, the reporter revealed that I had, in fact, been listening to Andy Murray talking about his Wimbledon prospects.

Jeremy Nicholas
Great Bardfield, Essex

SIR – No wonder Andy Murray rarely smiles even when winning a game. Just a glance at his support team is depressing enough. They look as if they are auditioning for an episode of *The Glums*.

Joan Abbs
Bury St Edmunds, Suffolk

SIR – Much as I do not wish to place any further pressure on the only real 'British' hope since Fred Perry, perhaps I could encourage the Braveheart from north of the border to adopt the new talisman of shaving. Not doing so has not worked so far.

R.A.
Manchester

DODGY DOUBLES

SIR — Sometimes the doubles players at Wimbledon look like a couple of cheap spivs trying to fix a particularly dodgy deal. I should love to pick up what they are actually saying:

'Crouch down and keep your bum low down as I'm going to serve to the right corner.'

'Don't forget it's your turn to do the washing up and cook the dinner later.'

'You owe me £5.50 for your share of the taxi fare here.'

David Horchover
Eastcote, Middlesex

SIR — What a pleasure to watch the Ladies' match between Rus and Stosur. Barely a groan throughout many hard-hitting exchanges. That racket should be confined to the boudoir.

M. Johnston
Oxted, Surrey

SIR – I haven't seen Pippa Middleton at Wimbledon today. Has she been knocked out?

David Brinkman
Poole, Dorset

SIR – I think David Nalbandian would have enjoyed a laugh if the line judges at his first match had walked on to the court wearing batsman's cricket pads. Matt could have done a good cartoon, too (apologies if he did and I missed it).

Martin Ranson
Thame, Oxfordshire

WELL DONE, FEDERER

SIR – Am I alone in being secretly pleased that Andy Murray lost?

Daniel Deasy
Oxford

SIR – When Fred Perry won a match he leapt over the net and shook the loser's hand. Nowadays, it seems, the winner flings himself to the ground and lies down, while the loser is reduced to tears. What a strange and weepy country we have become.

Peter Moore
Snelston, Derbyshire

SIR – I wouldn't cry if I received half a million pounds for losing a game of bat and ball.

Bill Clarke
South Chailey, East Sussex

SIR – As soon as I heard that David Cameron was backing Andy Murray I knew he would lose. Sure enough, Murray started off well but then did a U-turn.

Russ King
London N11

SIR – I was glad Alex Salmond was in the audience – he should remember to take Murray with him when Scotland gets its independence.

Philip Howells
Worsley, Lancashire

SIR – At least Andy Murray has some consolation

following his defeat — he'll now be Scottish again.

J.W.
Aberdeen

SIR — Can I assume that if Andy Murray were a horse, the Queen might have felt it incumbent upon her to attend the final at Wimbledon?

Daphne Marks
Radlett, Hertfordshire

SIR — When did the craze for instant interviewing after a sporting event begin? At the next Coronation, perhaps Clare Balding will be on hand at the Abbey to ask: 'How did the anointing go, your Majesty?'

We could also have surgeons emerging from theatre to deal with: 'Just take us through the difficulties of removing Tracy's spleen.'

Edward Thomas
Eastbourne, East Sussex

SIR — I'm assuming those people criticising Andy Murray's lack of ability and big-match mentality are the second or third best in the world in their own profession?

Mark Piggott
London N19

TOUR DE LONDRES

SIR – Congratulations to Bradley Wiggins on winning the Tour de France. Will he now perform a victory ride from Trafalgar Square to Waterloo Station?

M.G.
Guildford, Surrey

SIR – Congratulations to Bradley Wiggins. He has inspired me to retrieve my penny-farthing from the cellar, so that I can once more enjoy the pleasures of cycling around the highways and byways.

Ivor Yeloff
Hethersett, Norfolk

SIR – Bradley Wiggins is to be congratulated for his outstanding skill at cycling. Now if he could use his fame to make cyclists obey traffic laws, he would truly deserve a knighthood.

Caryl Roberts
Tattenhall, Cheshire

LEATHER ON SNOWY WILLOW

SIR – I passed Frome Cricket Club on a run in the winter and spotted five teenage lads practising in the nets, undeterred by the snow. Their perseverance ensures the future of the glorious game.

Rebecca Eleanor
Frome, Somerset

SIR – My wife and I have been watching the Test Match between New Zealand and South Africa at Dunedin. What a refreshing departure from the character of so much televised cricket! Nobody in the crowd wearing idiotic costumes, shouting, chanting, dancing or playing musical instruments – just people watching the cricket and applauding good play by either side.

How dull, some would say; but how civilised.

J.R.G. Edwards
Birchington, Kent

SIR – It is all very well our Test team claiming to be number one in the world but when they are beaten they fall back on insinuation. The action of the spinner Saeed Ajmal was cleared by Australian experts, and yet the England team continue to 'have their own opinions' as they cannot pick his doosra.

The reality is that they batted as if they could not pick a strawberry.

Stuart M. Archer
Batley, West Yorkshire

THE REAL SUMMER OF SPORT

SIR – Olympics! Olympics! Olympics! Let me make one thing absolutely clear: this year's truly great sporting contest begins on Thursday at the Oval. This isn't women's netball or synchronised swimming or some other meaningless activity. It's a three-match Test series between the top two teams in the world to determine which is number one.

Forget the Olympic opening and closing ceremonies and the bit in between. England winning at cricket is all that matters.

Ian Gill
Great Ouseburn, North Yorkshire

SIR – We are told that sitting down is bad for us. And yet in the next weeks we can watch the Open Golf; the Test Match; the Tour de France and the Olympics.

What can one do?

Douglas Barker
Beeston, Nottinghamshire

OLYMPIC COUNTDOWN

SIR – I am very concerned when the media describe the forthcoming Olympic Games as a 'once in a lifetime event'. I attended the 1948 London Olympics.

Roly Cockman
Horseheath, Cambridgeshire

SIR – Will someone please start a countdown to the *end* of the Olympics?

Rex Dixon
Marske-by-Sea, North Yorkshire

SIR – Lloyds bank has said that the 'happiness effect' of the Olympics is equivalent to each member of the population being given £165. Given the choice I'd take the money.

Peter Walton
Saxilby, Lincolnshire

SIR – Eight years ago Greece hosted the Olympics. When should we start to worry?

David Armstrong
Hipperholme, West Yorkshire

SIR – It's just like the end of the Roman Empire. We've had the bread, now the circuses and the Germans are just waiting to finish us off.

M.J. King
Amersham, Buckinghamshire

SIR – Given the overly zealous use of copyright law, will the phrase 'five gold rings' have to be omitted from the carol 'Twelve Days of Christmas'?

P.B.
Harbury, Warwickshire

SIR – Given the Government's predilection for awarding contracts to companies with names such as A4E and G4S, I am considering applying for funding to start up my own. I will be calling it Money4Me.

David Lysons
Gravesend, Kent

SIR – Is LOCOG an abbreviation of Low Cognitive Ability?

J.F. Collins
Groby, Leicestershire

SIR – If the East Enders don't want the missiles on their roof, can I please have them? The jackdaws are a damn nuisance down here.

Jeremy Brittain-Long
Constantine, Devon

OH, DANNY BOYLE

SIR – Brilliant. Bonkers. Oh, Danny Boyle, I loved it so.

Susy Goodwin
Ware, Hertfordshire

SIR – There is nothing like an Olympic Opening Ceremony to blow away cynicism.

Ben Crompton
Odiham, Hampshire

SIR – I have watched 10 minutes of the opening ceremony and am now leaving the country.

Christopher Hanson
Cheadle Hulme, Cheshire

SIR – Am I alone in thinking: What was that?

Dr David Jenkins
Ferryside, Carmarthenshire

SIR – Am I alone in thinking that Prince William waves like a girl?

M.C. Matson
Wass, North Yorkshire

SIR – After the Queen's spectacular film debut, can we now expect to see her take over the role of M from Dame Judi Dench?

E. McClung
Eastbourne, East Sussex

SIR – My mother rang me today from her house on the island of Kos in the Greek Dodecanese to ask whether it was true that the Queen did actually parachute into the Olympic stadium.

She tells me that following a news report on Greek television, the locals are convinced that she did and that she is amazing for her age.

David Lysons
Gravesend, Kent

SIR – It is heart-warming to know that although standards of care in the NHS may be slipping, our staff are such good dancers.

Dr Robert Walker
Great Clifton, Cumbria

SIR – Paul McCartney could sing; Sir Paul McCartney can't. Make him a Lord and perhaps he will stop.

Robert Plummer
Milborne Port, Somerset

BOTTOMLESS OLYMPIC PIN-UPS

SIR – I recently came across the word 'callipygous'. My edition of Chambers defines it marvellously as 'fair-buttocked', although I have also seen the rather more mundane 'having a beautiful bottom'.

Given the interest in beach volleyball, is it not time for the word to become more widely used? Perhaps there could be a gold medal for the most callipygous competitor?

Mark D. Wentworth
Netheravon, Wiltshire

SIR – If the women in the beach volleyball must wear bikinis, the men should wear Speedos. Seeing them in baggy shorts and T-shirts is very disappointing. I had held the Olympic ideal in higher esteem.

Sue Doughty
Twyford, Berkshire

SIR – If I remember the 2012 London Olympics for nothing else, I will remember them as the time Boris Johnson appeared on national television sporting his first decent haircut.

Valerie Moore
Lhanbryde, Moray

LOFTY OLYMPIC CONUNDRUMS

SIR – Instead of continually trying to find extraordinarily tall people for basketball teams, why don't they just lower the basket?

John McLennan
Coventry

SIR – Is there any truth to the theory that keirin cycle racing actually came about by mixing an appropriated moped; a large roundabout; a group of men away from home on a sports tour; and alcohol?

John Greenwood
Roxton, Bedfordshire

SIR – I thought hockey was played on grass. Also, why are there no mixed hockey matches in the Olympics? My wife and I met in such circumstances.

John Harvey
Budleigh Salterton, Devon

SIR – With all the sophisticated engineering projects that have gone towards making for a successful Olympics, surely it should no longer be beyond man's ability to design a garden strimmer that actually works?

Dr Alan Jones
Bryn-y-Gwenin, Monmouthshire

HIGH ON VICTORY

SIR – My wife and I decided to open a bottle of wine every time GB won a gold medal. A mistake.

Tony Hart
Ascot, Berkshire

SIR – I really can't wait for the Olympics to be over; all this welling-up with pride is exhausting.

Andrew Johnston
Wykey, Shropshire

SIR – Does anyone else find themselves humming 'Chariots of Fire' at inopportune moments?

Penny Hurley
Dunmow, Essex

SIR — As a dual citizen of Australia and Britain for some 18 years, I have this week decided to fully embrace my Britishness. This, of course, has nothing to do with these countries' medal standings.

Stephen Hay
St Helier, Jersey

SIR — Perhaps Cadbury's should produce a special selection of chocolate coins, to give the Australians something to take home.

Alex Perry
Thames Ditton, Surrey

SIR —
'Bradley Wiggins'.
Is an 'American'.
'Double'.
'Backed' also by London ****.
A 'Double'?
YOU KNOW.
Because I 'e-mailed'.
'The Sun' about this issue.
Yesterday.
And you KNEW about this.
Before printing your 'rag'.
LIARS.
For 'American'.
MONEY.
Your 'rag'.

Which the new 'C' has to read.
So YOU.
Have to 'go'.
Sorry ...
cc BIG BROTHER
B.O.S.S.
MI9
GCHQ
22 SAS
MI5
MI7
Control
The Circus
M

BBC ALSO-RANS

SIR – Will someone please ask the BBC to desist from the inane questioning of disappointed, breathless competitors, who have trained for years and are hardly at their best post-event? The interviews are insensitive and evidently wounding.

Perhaps the producers will ask themselves if they would like to be asked about their own examination failures which resulted in their careers in television.

J.B. Shrive
Holt, Norfolk

MEDDAW TALLY

SIR – Have you noticed the number of competitors and commentators who refer to Gold, Silver and Bronze *meddaws*? Some are hoping to *meddaw*, some wish to be *meddawing* and others will have *meddaws* thrust upon them.

Brian Empringham
Ilfracombe, Devon

SIR – I watched swimming from the Olympics today and saw that it was broadcast from the Aquatics Centre. What has happened to the swimming pool?

Christopher Boyle
Milton Keynes, Buckinghamshire

THE USE AND
ABUSE OF
LANGUAGE

LOST FOR DICTIONARIES

SIR – I have just returned from a visit to my local library. To my astonishment the library staff were unable to provide me with a dictionary in English. Words fail me – and the library staff likewise, I assume.

Stuart Shaw
Stockport

DRIVEN TO DAMNATION

SIR – On rare occasions, there are some people, such as car drivers, queue jumpers and football referees, who so infuriate me that I want to respond verbally. While completely denigrating any outburst that could be deemed racist, sexist, ageist, and the rest, how does one insult someone without falling foul of the Morality Police?

'Silly devil' doesn't really work.

J. Wright
Hull

SIR – When I left school, my House Tutor's final words of wisdom included: 'Swearing is acceptable as long as one does not use any word which contains the letter "u".'

A simple formula to remember for the last 58 years.

John White
Over Stowey, Somerset

HI, AMERICA

SIR – When I remonstrated with a friend over her use of 'Hi' at the beginning of an email she replied that 'it is standard email procedure'. Really? And who sets the standard? No doubt the United States. If I fail to use it will I be *hi*-tailed to America under the notorious Extradition Act?

A.H.
Minchinhampton, Gloucestershire

SIR – My wife and I recently returned from a very enjoyable holiday in the Cotswolds. How dispiriting, though, to be greeted at a quintessential village pub with, 'Hi, guys'.

Tim Barnaby
Preesall, Lancashire

SIR – Can we not find an English expression to replace the increasing use of the phrase 'stepping up to the plate'? We do not play baseball here to any great extent, for which we must be grateful.

Peter Thompson
Sutton, Surrey

SIR – I am fed up with people calling children 'kids'. Our children are children, not goats.

Rosanne Levett-Scrivener
Sibton, Suffolk

SIR – In a British court there is no stand, there is a witness box. It is not taken, it is entered.

M.R.H.
Monmouth

SIR – Sadly I am becoming immune to Americanisms such as 'train station' (even used in the *Telegraph*), the pronunciation of the letter 'h' in Anthony and the stressing of the second syllable in 'Bernard' and 'Maurice'. Yet even I was shocked to see that at Aliwal Barracks, Tidworth, the British Army possesses something called the 1st Mechanized Brigade.

Presumably they all walk about chewing gum and saluting with their hats off.

Steven Broomfield
Fair Oak, Hampshire

DIEU PROTÈGE LA REINE

SIR – I see that all immigrants will have to learn the national anthem as part of the new citizenship test. Will the Government ease this task by having it translated into a dozen other languages, as with other official documents?

Alan Shaw
Halifax, West Yorkshire

SIR – I see that foreign languages will be made compulsory in schools from the age of seven. Living in a multi-ethnic, multi-lingual area of West Yorkshire, might I suggest English as the language of choice?

Maureen Scatchard
Batley, West Yorkshire

GR8 SPELING

SIR – My nine-year-old granddaughter Molly
was ever so proud of the certificate awarded by
her school for reaching the final of a spelling
contest. The certificate bore the legend 'spelling
competetion'(sic) – and this at what is considered to
be a very good school.

Alan Murphy
East Cowton, North Yorkshire

SIR – Perhaps we could start to improve teenagers'
spelling by banning the use of the quaint, but
patently inaccurate, term 'the three Rs'.

T.S.
Oxford

SIR – I taught both my children their times tables
by singing them while doing aerobics to a Carol
Vorderman times table video. I remember it well,
especially Carol's knee-length leather boots.

A.J.
Syston, Leicestershire

SIR – Of the 15 condolence letters I received,
having recently been bereaved, no fewer than eight
addressed the envelope without using the title of Mr
or Esq. Six of them were from friends and relatives

under the age of 25. I wonder whether this is through ignorance or now the current trend.

R.M.
Westcliff-on-Sea, Essex

RECORD PEDANTS

SIR – In an article about knotweed today you quote Lord Taylor thus: 'Research is going on into a leaf spot fungus which also has the capacity to very specifically, and this of course is the key to biological control, attack Japanese knotweed.'

Pace Fowler and Partridge, we pedants can spot a split infinitive from 100 yards. Yet a split infinitive usually comprises just three words. The good Lord Taylor has concocted one comprising 14 words. Is this a record?

Barry Ryder
Coggeshall, Essex

SIR – I was appalled to hear David Cameron say in an interview yesterday, 'What drives the Deputy Prime Minister and I . . .'

I am surprised that he didn't add 'innit' at the end of the sentence.

Bill Malloy
New Duston, Northamptonshire

SIR — Am I alone in becoming increasingly exasperated when politicians, broadcasters and columnists confuse *less* with *fewer* and *amount* with *number*? Or do these things not matter anymore?

Patrick Briggs
Cambridge

SIR — It is regrettable that the latest television advertisement for Marks and Spencer mentions a 'most unique' item. Some years ago M&S led the food retailers in knowing the difference between *less* and *fewer* when describing how many items were acceptable in a basket at the checkout.

Peter Whitehead
Blackpool

SIR — Your correspondent is right when he says that we are losing many of our prepositions, but he must have noticed that they are being replaced by one all-purpose preposition: *around*. All 'issues' nowadays are 'around' something or other; legislation is framed 'around' particular fields.

People who are attempting to sound posh, however, will often substitute the word *surrounding*.

B.E.
Manchester

SIR – Am I alone in being afraid to communicate, both verbally and in writing, after reading Simon Heffer's excellent book *Strictly English*?

B. Hart
Hemswell, Lincolnshire

SIR – I wonder if those who decry grammar would like to live in houses built by people with little knowledge of their components or how to assemble them into a coherent structure.

Geoffrey Hodgson
Shadwell, West Yorkshire

UNUSUAL ARCHITECTS

SIR – Several years ago an agent gave us details of a house 'designed by an architect with many unusual features'.

Sue Beresford
Chalfont St Giles, Buckinghamshire

SIR – What is 'sustainable house building'? One cannot eat brickwork.

Eric Saunders
Crawley Down, West Sussex

SIR – Does anyone in the Socialist Workers' Party work?

Jim Parker
Bristol

SIR – Is there an organisation more inappropriately named than Unite?

Lawrence Fraser
Elgin, Moray

SIR – When I was teaching, I once received a note from a pupil's mother asking for her daughter to be excused PE 'as she is under the doctor with her legs'.

David Partington
Higher Walton, Cheshire

SIR – Our cruise to the Red Sea was cancelled, with only five days' notice and without explanation. Costa apologised for 'the incontinence that this has caused you'.

A.W.
Upper Brailes, Oxfordshire

SIR – I recently bought a replacement windscreen wiper blade. After declining the fitting service I followed the instructions. These, in their entirety, read: 'Remove the old blade. Fit the new blade.'

As a once technical author and editor, I must commend the writer on the economy of words.

P. Joy
East Chelborough, Dorset

THE PC DICTIONARY

SIR – I see that *fatty* is to be deemed a 'hate' word. Presumably *skinny*, *lofty*, *shorty*, *carrot-top* and *baldy* will also be included.

Perhaps a dictionary guide could be published to aid us all as to which descriptive words are considered illegal.

Geoff Higgs
Eastcote, Middlesex

SIR – I agree that doctors using the word *obese* could be unhelpful. They should tell the patient that he or she is *fat*. This would provide a clearer understanding of the situation.

Jim Wilkinson
Great Coates, Lincolnshire

SIR – The Bishop of Bath and Wells says that the rioters were finding 'spiritual release'. I thought they were finding trainers and televisions.

John Pini
Stamford, Lincolnshire

SIR – No more 'Baa Baa Black Sheep', but 'Baa Baa Little Sheep'. This means that if my family consider my lifestyle outrageous, I shall have to become the little sheep of the family, which, considering that I weigh 17 stone, seems a touch inaccurate.

I shouldn't really complain, though; if we are to consider the original epithet, neither am I black.

Dr John Gladstone
Gerrards Cross, Buckinghamshire

IT'S NOT ABOUT THE GETTING A RESULT

SIR – According to Roy Hodgson, England 'got a result' against Ukraine. His statement makes me as sick as a parrot. Why could he not bring himself to say 'we won'?

Andrew Blake
Shalbourne, Wiltshire

SIR — Another year of Wimbledon, another year of tennis players *crashing out* of the tournament. Ridiculous turn of phrase.

Nick Allen
Singapore

SIR — I find it increasingly irritating to hear *card* in golf, as in so-and-so *carded* a score of 72.

Sandra Janes
Praa Sands, Cornwall

SIR — Misuse of the word *literally* is not new; about 20 years ago I heard a horse racing commentator saying, 'They will literally be getting out of their graves to back this one.'

John G. Prescott
Coulsdon, Surrey

SIR — I think the Liberal Democrats are *literally* finished.

M.B.
Crosby, Merseyside

TOUGH LISTENS

SIR — A contributor to this morning's *Today* programme confessed that something was a 'tough listen'. It is bad enough when people complain that difficult questions are a 'hard ask'. When is all this 'nouning up' going to end?

C.B.
Milton Keynes, Buckinghamshire

SIR – I almost choked on my cornflakes when I heard someone proclaim that they had 'breakfasted' their children.

Dr C.J. Fletcher
Stanton St John, Oxfordshire

SIR – Please don't get me started on nouns being used as verbs. My own bête noir is the use of verbs as nouns, and in particular the use of the verb *invite* as a noun. Insult is added to injury by placing the emphasis on the first syllable.

Jennifer Adams
London SW11

SIR – While listening to the radio this morning the announcer said that something was 'trending'. What on earth does that mean?

Roger Bruce
Tadworth, Surrey

SIR – Do other readers share my irritation that during an interview, the only current reply to any question is 'Absolutely'? Even our Prime Minister was guilty of the constant use of this horrible word on the *Today* programme this morning.

Stephanie Cooper-Chadwick
London W12

SIR – Could someone please explain the difference between 'Thanks', 'Thank you', 'Thank you very much' and 'Thank you very much indeed' so beloved of our radio interviewers?

Guy Arnoux
Wells, Somerset

SIR – My blood pressure soars to a dangerous level every time I am informed that so-and-so has 'appeared' on radio; this is plainly impossible.

M.S.
London SE23

SIR – Congratulations to *BBC Breakfast's* Bill Turnbull on correctly pronouncing the surname Brontë on this morning's programme. Why is this name so frequently mispronounced as 'Brontay'?

Angie Sello
Woodbridge, Suffolk

SIR – Regrettably it has become commonplace to hear words ending in 'ing' mispronounced as though they end with the letter 'k'. While listening to a recent morning service on Radio 4 I was somewhat taken aback to hear the minister solemnly intone the passage from 1 Corinthians 15:55, 'O death, where is thy stink?'

John Jarman
Ramsey, Isle of Man

SIR – Why have BBC television actors ceased to speak English, substituting it for inaudible Mumblish? Could it be that it saves having to learn their lines? I am returning to books.

Edward Le Besque
Burwash, East Sussex

SIR – I was prompted to write this after hearing a not very pleasant pronunciation on the radio:

Since when did book rhyme with buck?
Or indeed look with luck?
I don't give a fook for the best written book
If reviewed by a girl who says 'buck'.

Thank you.
Gay Hamilton
London NW6

SIR – I fear that the cuts in the BBC have not gone far enough. On their website I found the following: 'The British Library is examining how our landscapes have permeated 150 great literary works – influencing and shaping writers' proses (sic).'

I wonder if the writer of this piece had read any of those 'great works'.

John Doran
London W13

SIR – The Beeb's latest affectation? 'Jubi-*lee*', with the stress on the last syllable.

J.B. Norman
Exmouth, Devon

WHAT A SHOWER!

SIR – The attractive young lady presenting ITV's weather informed us that there will be 'showery rain' today. I wonder when we will be having shiny sun and breezy wind.

June Brown
Lytham, Lancashire

SIR – Why are hailstones always the size of golf balls? Do they come in any other sizes?

Gareth Temple
Kessingland, Suffolk

SIR – What annoys me is when a weather reporter, having talked about low *temritures,* tells us to 'wrap up warm'. It is an adverb. It is *warmly.*

G.P.
Cranbrook, Kent

SIR – My wish is for a filter to be used during the weather forecast, removing all of the following: 'odd rumble of thunder'; 'temperatures really struggling'; 'head through' – as a reference to the passage of time; 'a wet old day'; all references to the weather being 'out there' (where else would it be?); unwanted value judgements, especially disapproval of rain; reminders that the BBC has its own website.

Ben Elford
Clutton, Somerset

SIR – Can someone tell weather forecasters that there is a 't' in Scotland?

Michael Brotherton
Chippenham, Wiltshire

THE DAILY DICTIONARY

SIR – One knows one is reading a quality newspaper when it requires a visit to the dictionary in the course of reading an article. This week it was *sophistical* in Dr Theodore Dalrymple's article.

J.McL.
Coventry

SIR – Yesterday's paper quoted the American actress, Goldie Hawn, saying: 'We need to habituate better thinking to appreciate more of your day because that has a neurological correlate.'

Can anyone translate this for me?

B.L.
Verwood, Dorset

SIR – I do enjoy Boris Johnson's Monday article – and indeed his televised machinations at the London Assembly – but I would enjoy it even more if I did not have to resort to the OED or Google to find the meanings of some of his more abstruse words and phrases. Today it was 'poujadiste revolt'.

Keep things simple, please, Boris. Or am I alone in my ignorance?

Dr Barry Doran
Stockport

SIR — It is time that the *Telegraph* knew the difference between a cross and a crucifix (I am really disappointed that even Boris Johnson doesn't seem to know). A crucifix carries the figure of Christ, a cross does not, so the words are not interchangeable.

Elizabeth Morland
Stanford in the Vale, Oxfordshire

SIR — Can you get your correspondents to use the word *decimate* properly? Twice last week it was used to mean 'destroy'.

Edward Baker
Tunbridge Wells, Kent

SIR — In all that is being written about high pay, bonuses and other excessive emoluments, I do wish journalists would avoid writing that anyone *earns* such sums. They may be paid them, they may receive them or they may have them thrust into their unwilling hands, but if they do not deserve them, they cannot be said to earn them.

It is a little word, and therefore attractive to sub-editors, but it should be avoided.

T.B.
Bognor Regis, West Sussex

SIR — How long does someone have to be dead before people stop saying 'the late'? I note that Lord

Longford was referred to as such recently, and yet he has been dead for some years. Nobody would say 'the late William Shakespeare'. Are there rules to this?

R.F.
Carlus, Midi-Pyrénées, France

SIR – Oh dear, things have come to a pretty pass when the leader writer of the *Telegraph* writes *testament* for *testimony* and *mix* for *mixture*. You're supposed to be setting standards, not joining in the general slide toward their obliteration.

M.D'A.
London W8

SIR – A mere four inches from a letter headed 'Horrible new verb' (the content of which can only be met with agreement) is your leader writer's trendy and equally annoying misuse of a real verb. Babies, parcels and speeches can be *delivered*, what the Government wants from train operating companies cannot.

Andrew Bennett
Derby

HALF-WITTED OVERHEARD CONVERSATIONS

SIR – Following the first landing on the moon in 1969, I overheard two colleagues discussing the event. After acknowledging the seminal feat, one concluded her remarks by commenting: 'What made it all the more remarkable was that it was only a half moon at the time.'

Josephine Hinson
Gurnard, Isle of Wight

SIR – I once saw an elderly lady pointing to the sundial in Nelson's Dockyard, Antigua, and saying, 'Fancy, it still keeps good time after all these years.'

R.P.
Newark, Nottinghamshire

SIR – I have always wondered what, in the late 1960s, prompted someone to write on the wall of a public lavatory in a town in Lancashire, 'King Zog of Albania was a fool unto himself.'

Frank Wilkinson
Lostock, Lancashire

SIR – My family home, Compton Castle, built in the 14th century, is open to the public. For the convenience of the visitors, my father had a sign saying 'Lavatory' placed on a door. One day, my mother overheard a young man say to his companion, 'What's a lavatory, dear?' To which she replied, 'That's mediaeval for toilet.'

His Honour Judge Francis Gilbert, QC
Bovey Tracey, Devon

SIR – While towing my young children around the Pencil Museum in Keswick, I overheard two old dears who were looking at the prize exhibit, the world's longest coloured pencil. After studying it for some time, one said to the other: 'It's not very sharp, is it?'

The other replied, 'Well, if they keep sharpening it, it wouldn't be the world's longest pencil, would it?'

Incidentally, the Pencil Museum is only beaten for excitement by the Norwegian Canning Museum in Stavanger. Dedicated to all things relating to the canning of fish, its machinery operates on a Tuesday and a Thursday. Once smelt, never forgotten.

Christopher Harris
Ponteland, Northumberland

SIR – Some time ago my wife and I were admiring a splendid bog garden in the grounds of a Cornish hotel, which had superb examples of mature gunnera with their huge rhubarb-like foliage. From a few yards behind us, I overheard a mature lady saying to her friend, 'No, dear, it's not rhubarb, it's called gonorrhoea.'

Needless to say, we had to walk on before letting out a quiet snigger.

R.J.
North Devon

SIR – While walking in Paris, my wife and I passed a couple who were window shopping for some expensive jewellery. My wife heard the man say to the lady, 'I'd buy that for you, darling, but not for my wife.'

Roy Watkinson
Lewes, East Sussex

SIR – At a concert I attended recently, the man sitting in front of me said to his companion, 'You see that woman over there; isn't she ugly?'

His companion said, 'Oh, don't say that, it's cruel. She can't help it.'

'Yes, she can,' he replied. 'She could stay at home.'

John L. Fisher
Leeds

SIR – While standing on a bridge over the River Cam, I heard someone on a punt telling his passengers about the British Civil War.

John Chambers
Witham, Essex

SIR – Two dons were parking their bikes near the Bodleian in Oxford when one said to the other, 'And ninthly . . .'

Rosemary Morton Jack
Oddington, Oxfordshire

BLUE-SKY BINGO

SIR – Years ago there was a version of bingo much favoured by inveterate meeting-attenders at one of the professional bodies to which I have the honour to belong.

It consisted of cards containing 15 clichés and platitudes (such as 'blue-sky scenario' and 'Let's run this one up the flagpole and see who salutes it'). Our job was to cross off each one as it appeared. Anyone with the phrase 'going forward' on their card usually had a head start.

Dr Ted Johns
Odiham, Hampshire

SIR – When Jo Causon, Chief Executive of the Institute of Customer Service, called in her letter for banks to offer 'a jargon-free banking experience' and an 'enhanced overall service offering', was she being ironic?

Michael Perris
Brighton, East Sussex

INSIDIOUSLY ANNOYING PHRASES

SIR – There is an insidious movement afoot wherein statements or observations are prefaced with 'So'. Where does this come from and does it serve any purpose other than to irritate intensely?

Paul Latcham
Hereford

SIR – Does anyone take any notice of the phrase 'lessons must be learned' or is it the most useless phrase in the English language?

Dorothy Arnold
Shrivenham, Oxfordshire

SIR – Am I alone in hoping that the fashionable use of the term 'pop-up' (as in shop, studio and restaurant) is just a temporary thing?

John Hughes
Nailsea, Somerset

SIR – When and why did the horrible expression 'rent out' come into being?

Elizabeth Prince
Littlehampton, West Sussex

SIR — Why is it that when you politely brush off a caller with whom you don't want to speak, they always say 'Not a problem' before putting down the phone? It may not be one for them, but it annoys the life out of me.

Rosie Inge
Bleadney, Somerset

SIR — Am I alone in becoming increasingly irritated, to the point of annoyance, by a new trend of being asked 'How are you today?' by service suppliers when cold calling me on the telephone?

Is this a genuine enquiry to hear my list of ailments? Or is the question an inane way of trying to bond with a prospective customer?

I find myself trying to move on the conversation with as much politeness as I can conjure up in the trying circumstances.

John Harvey
Budleigh Salterton, Devon

SIR — Despite my best efforts to keep up to date with changes in the use of English, I just cannot get used to the apparently universal, 'I'm good' in reply to 'How are you?' It does my head in. Innit.

Andrew Lakeman
Pensford, Somerset

SIR — Could someone please tell me how and when the word *unvalued* came into the English language. I appreciate that language has to 'live', but does it really need to be so debased?

Margaret Malcolm
Churchdown, Gloucestershire

HACKINGLY BAD PUNS

SIR — I hear that Rebekah Brooks borrowed a police horse from the Met. Was it a hack?

B.F.
Dunbar, East Lothian

SIR — The Leveson Inquiry is rapidly degenerating into a Nags-to-Bitches story.

R.S.
Goudhurst, Kent

SIR — I was disturbed by your headline, 'Baroness never paid for her stays'. Must we poke our noses into peers' undergarments?

C.H-E.
Northwood, Middlesex

SIR – Was I alone in finding Justin Webb's comment on the *Today* programme about breast implant clinics 'going bust' amusing? It did make me titter.

D.M.
Hitchin, Hertfordshire

SIR – Five or more pages devoted to Andy Murray, but not a mention of Jonny Marray – is this latest example of U and non-U?

J.P.
Ross-on-Wye, Herefordshire

SIR – The opening of 'The Making of Harry Potter' has left me puzzled. Mr and Mrs Potter should be centre stage, and yet do not even seem to warrant a mention.

A.P.
Thames Ditton, Surrey

SIR – This morning I witnessed a large number of silver-haired drivers waiting patiently for the privilege of paying 143.9p for a litre of petrol. Does this confirm that there is no fuel like an old fuel?

D.O.
Pilley, Hampshire

THE ROADS MUCH TRAVELLED

HIGH-SPEED SINGLES

SIR — I can readily see why someone would want to leave Birmingham as fast as possible, but I do not understand why any sane person would want to get there sooner. So I have a simple suggestion to halve the cost of HS2: build just one railway line out of Brum.

Robert Warner
West Woodhay, Berkshire

SIR — Passengers on HS2 will actually waste more time as their mobile phones and laptops will not work in the planned tunnels.

Alison Hamilton
Wigginton, Oxfordshire

SIR — I recall that a full English breakfast on trains from Euston to Birmingham New Street could be enjoyed and digested during the 85 minute journey. I doubt this will be the case during a 45 minute journey.

David Cooper
Effingham, Surrey

SIR — In the light of the Government's announcements of additional tunnels along the HS2 route, should an objector now be referred to as a

NUMPTY (Not Underneath My Patio, Thank You)?

Richard Cleaver
Stamford, Lincolnshire

iDESPAIR OF YOUR MUSIC

SIR – For a company that prides itself on the quality of its products, Apple's standard headphones included with every i-device are an absolute disgrace. If Steve Jobs, God rest his soul, had ever the misfortune to sit next to someone using a pair on a lengthy train journey, I am convinced heads would have rolled in Cupertino, California.

R.S.
Burgess Hill, West Sussex

SIR – Should eating crisps in a quiet carriage be allowed?

Andy Krasun
Broughton, Hampshire

SIR – What on earth has happened to cotton handkerchiefs, preferably with a rolled edge, on the Tube and elsewhere?

John M. Whalley
Longridge, Lancashire

SIR – I am seriously worried. Since you published my letter regarding lack of investment in our railways, my regular train home from London has been short of four carriages, forcing us to be crammed like battery hens. How did they know which train I was on?

Ian Rennardson
Hildenborough, Kent

TEXTING ON THE ORIENT EXPRESS

SIR – Your picture of the incident in which a train hit a patch of mud in Fife, injuring none of the 32 on board, shows at least six police officers, one of whom appears to be texting.

How did Poirot manage to cope with the Murder on the Orient Express on his own?

Gordon Black
Kilmarnock, East Ayrshire

WELCOME TO BRITAIN

SIR – On Boxing Day my half-hour train journey from the centre of Berlin to the airport cost me three Euros. During the flight back to Luton, passengers were informed that a train fare into

London would cost £14 and that when they arrived, there would be no Underground service owing to a tube strike. Welcome home!

Richard Hill
Diss, Norfolk

SIR – Someone asked on Twitter if anyone knew of cheap overnight accommodation at Gatwick. I suggested the immigration queues.

Steve Cattell
Hougham, Lincolnshire

SIR – What is the point of the Government telling the UK Border Agency that its employees must be smart, if they are allowed to sit in front of the waiting passengers at Stansted and Luton chewing gum like a bunch of yobs?

John Alborough
Syleham, Suffolk

SIR – May I suggest that the reason passport checks are not carried out on the Eurostar train is because a goodly proportion of their passengers travel under it.

Peter Dobbie
Edith Weston, Rutland

SIR – With the discovery of a terrorist plot to blow up planes using underwear bombs, will we soon have to pass through airports wearing no underwear?

P.H.
Terling, Essex

SIR – The reason wasps and bees kill more people than terrorists is that they don't have to go through airport security.

Robert Guttridge
Sheffield

SIR – If bees are more efficient at killing us than terrorists, they should be trained to turn their attention to the terrorists.

John Hall
St Neots, Cambridgeshire

SIR – My grandmother, who was born in 1887, always referred to Heathrow as 'the London Airplane Station'.

Angela Clifford
Epsom, Surrey

ON HER MAJESTY'S POTHOLE SERVICE

SIR – I have just received a very polite letter from Harrogate's highways department informing me of the impending inconvenience of pothole patching in the village. The most charming part of the letter tells me that if I should encounter any problems, 'Traffic Ambassadors' will be on hand to assist motorists.

How do I identify these ambassadors? Will they be in pinstripes and hi-vis bowlers? Will they have diplomatic immunity to avoid the wrath of the motorists seething with anger behind me while I ask for the latest detour to the supermarket?

If only more brown envelopes that thump on the mat could raise such a smile.

L.R. Carter
Markington, North Yorkshire

SIR – I see that the City of Westminster now calls its traffic wardens Civil Enforcement Officers. In future I shall inquire a little more closely when someone tells me that he is a 'CEO in the City'.

Gavin Choyce
London W2

SIR – I have a suggestion with regards to the enormous problem of potholes on our roads: bring back chain gangs.

John Harvey
Budleigh Salterton, Devon

DOWN AT THE END OF LONELY STREET

SIR – I had a favourite pub in the village of Newington Bagpath. After an enjoyable evening, I would drive my girlfriend home via Ozleworth Bottom, through Synwell to Breakheart Hill, which in the light of subsequent events was aptly named.

Colin Cummings
Yelvertoft, Northamptonshire

SIR – Driving through Lincolnshire once we saw a signpost: 'To Mavis Enderby and Old Bolingbroke', underneath which some wag had added, '. . . a son'.

Sue Lister
West Horndon, Essex

SIR – Should not the East Sussex village of Upper Dicker be twinned with Muff in Monaghan in the Irish Republic?

Paul Codrington
Minster-on-Sea, Isle of Sheppey

SIR – Definitely not for publication: Velvet Bottom with Tongue End.

M.H.
Milton Keynes

THE TOUCH OF FROST

SIR – Most cars these days have heated rear screens. Some have heated windscreens and heated mirrors. Some even have heated seats. So why do so few, if any, have heated steering wheels to warm the driver's cold hands on frosty mornings?

Terry Lloyd
Darley Abbey, Derbyshire

SIR – My father had a friend who, each evening before winter weather was predicted, would fastidiously place a newspaper over the windscreen of his vehicle. The next morning he would set fire to the newspaper, thus resulting in a nice clear screen, and off he would go.

An old army trick, I believe.

Elliot T. Wilson
Scarborough, North Yorkshire

SURVIVAL OF THE MAP READERS

SIR – An article on page two today explained how the human race is still evolving by natural selection. On page seven there was a report about a couple driving into a river because their sat-nav told them to.

Jeremy Coleman
Hinxton, Essex

SIR – I have no use for a sat-nav. I always rely upon the Mark One Human Brain v. 1946. This is constantly updated, in real time, using twin ocular instruments, corrected for astigmatism with a handy piece of hardware.

The whole system uses the common sense and intelligence software package in conjunction with a portable version of the current map operating system.

If that doesn't work, I have an infallible back-up system – my wife tells me where to go.

Roy Hughes
Bromsgrove, Worcestershire

SCOOTER COMING THROUGH

SIR — I was much amused by the Duke of Edinburgh asking a gentleman on a mobility scooter how many people he'd knocked over. Having recently had to resort to one, I could write a book on the hazards of navigating around people on the narrow pavements of a busy town centre. And as for the young lady doing a hop, skip and jump with her ears plugged into a music device, it took two van drivers shouting and my (rather weak) horn to get her to move.

J.S. Carter
Tunbridge Wells, Kent

SIR — Has anyone else noticed that on rainy days in busy towns, not only can cyclists sail through red traffic lights with immunity, they can also cycle using one hand to steer while holding an open umbrella with the other?

Janice Dark
West Wratting, Cambridgeshire

ROAD HOGS

SIR – With reference to your correspondent's inquiry, I have always understood that vehicles with darkened windows were driven by people with ugly children.

Sir Richard Dashwood Bt
Ledwell, Oxfordshire

SIR – Have you noticed that the bigger the car, the tubbier the driver and the passengers? Everywhere you see capacious tummies just clear of the airbags, podgy fingers clutching handbags, sour-faced, bouncing bosoms defiantly testing their stays, as they turbo-whirr their way in search of more grub to feed insatiable XXL appetites.

Joe Gibson Dawson
Withnell, Lancashire

SIR – Am I alone in being amazed by the number of vehicles which appear not to be fitted with direction indicators? My car has factory-fitted indicators as standard, and I find that they are incredibly simple to operate, and an easy way of letting other road users know in advance when I am proposing to turn left or right.

P.H. York
Daventry, Northamptonshire

ONE FOR THE FLIGHT

SIR – In the Gatwick departures lounge a shop
is giving away tasting samples of Californian
chardonnay at 8 a.m. I accept that airports, like
postmodern novels, are unbound by conventions
of nation or time, but surely everyone here is on
English time?

J. MacD.
West Sussex

THE BOOK LESS TRAVELLED

SIR – While rereading a book I will notice a spot of
sun tan oil from sunbathing on a Greek island; the
coffee stain which dropped while reading at a table
on a Parisian boulevard; and the small runnel of
peach juice which dribbled down while surveying a
scene in Tuscany. Can you do that when rereading a
book on Kindle? I think not!

Elisabeth Armstrong-Rosser
London NW6

HOME
THOUGHTS ON
ABROAD

CAPTAIN MULLET

SIR – Am I alone in being hair-ist? The captain of the Costa Concordia sports a mullet which is only a rubber band short of a ponytail. For me, that says it all.

Mark Prior
Crownhill, Devon

SIR – The course selected by Captain Francesco Schettino unfortunately had insufficient *offing* because of too much *showing offing*.

C.G.W. Wilks
Billesdon, Leicestershire

SIR – 'I tripped and fell into the lifeboat' is the most abject excuse since 'The dog ate my homework' and 'It was approved by the fees office'.

Dr John Doherty
Vienna, Austria

SIR – Can anyone explain to me why, in these enlightened times of equality, a woman has more right to a place in a lifeboat than a man?

T.O.
Lancaster

SIR – The actions of the Italian captain of the Costa Concordia bring to mind the experience of the Italian Military Band at the 1969 London Royal Tournament. The Band of the Bersaglieri always moves at the double and found the Earls Court sand a difficult surface. The Italian bandmaster complained to the British director stating, 'We cannot run on sand.' His reply, 'Well, it did not stop you in North Africa in 1940' resulted in what can only be described as a gap in the programme.

Lord Fermoy
Sibford Gower, Oxfordshire

FRENZIED EUROSCEPTICS

SIR – I used to describe myself as a political refugee from the Orwellian experiment that is the EU. Now, thanks to Ken Clarke's attack on those who want a referendum, I will proudly describe myself as a 'frenzied eurosceptic'.

Chris Watson
Tasmania, Australia

SIR – Following the Royal Bank of Scotland's problems with its online accounts, can we not turn misfortune to our advantage by putting them in charge of paying our £40 million-a-day membership fee to Brussels?

Richard Shaw
Dunstable, Bedfordshire

SIR – I recently overheard a shop assistant try to dissuade a customer from taking a carrier bag for her newspaper by saying, 'The EU is soon going to stop free plastic bags.'

I was bemused when the customer replied, 'They're always trying to stop your fun.'

Before free plastic bags disappear, can anybody tell me what fun I've been missing out on all these years?

Tim Barnsley
London SW16

FIGHTING GREEK FIRE WITH FIRE

SIR – Every four years Greece exports a magnificent flame to whichever country happens to be hosting the Olympic Games. Why don't they start charging for it?

C.M.
London N11

SIR – May I suggest that a more helpful contribution to resolving the Greek debt problem would be to stage the Olympic Games permanently in Greece?

Dr Nigel J. Knott
Farleigh Wick, Wiltshire

SIR – Cambridge and Oxford have a system whereby the rich colleges, in accordance with their relative wealth, contribute to a central fund from which the poor colleges receive, according to their relative poverty.

Could not the Eurozone be organised on the same lines?

Alexander Hopkinson-Woolley
Bembridge, Isle of Wight

SIR – How many haircuts can a Greek have before one realises he has no hair?

Gerald Josephs
London NW11

SIR – Perhaps Mykonos should sell Greece.

Dr Juan Carlos d'Abrera
Victoria, Australia

SIR — One is, of course, delighted to hear that the Greek economy is to be saved — once again.

On a recent visit to Crete I asked for the recipe for a Greek salad. There came the not entirely ironic reply, 'First, you borrow some feta . . .'

Christopher Rodda
Boscastle, Cornwall

SIR — Rather than returning to drachmas, Greece would be well advised to use doner kebabs, which are universally accepted and recognised as currency.

Jon Levenson
Hargrave, Cheshire

SIR — As a subscriber I recently received a calendar from you which showed February with six Thursdays and only two Sundays. Is this part of David Cameron's plan to get us out of the recession? Perhaps he could suggest this system to Greece to reduce their deficit — although the Greek Orthodox Church might complain as their collections will be down.

Roger Stones
Dorking, Surrey

SIR — As we await catastrophe in Greece, do we not need a fine statue in Parliament Square of

Gordon Brown who, whatever else one thinks of him, singlehandedly thwarted Tony Blair's insane desire to join the doomed Euro project?

Julian Le Vay
Oxford

SIR – Today I received a letter from The Pension Service telling me that I will now receive my state pension from the age of 66. I am going to file it with their previous letter telling me that my state pension would be paid once I reached 64 years and 10 months, and not at 60.

I'm thinking of moving to Greece because I know how they must be feeling.

Shirley Batten-Smith
Watford, Hertfordshire

L'ENTENTE MERDIQUE

SIR – Now that the 'Merkozy' alliance has been terminated by the French elections, will the new association be called 'Merde'?

Geoff Beecher
Amersham, Buckinghamshire

THE RECIPROCAL RELATIONSHIP

SIR – The unprecedented honour of a seat on Air Force One for the Prime Minister to accompany President Obama to a basketball game in Ohio calls for a reciprocal gesture if and when the President comes here again. A trip on a London bus to a football match at Brentford or Leyton Orient might be an appropriate gesture, sausage rolls provided at half-time.

Kenneth Wood
Exeter

SIR – If Mitt Romney becomes US President, how many First Ladies would he be allowed?

Adrian Markley
Salisbury

PENN FRIEND

SIR – I see Sean Penn's latest role is to intervene in the politics of the Falklands. I trust he demonstrates the same initiative in his own country and strives towards returning America to the Native American Indian.

Diane Queen
Henllan, Denbighshire

SIR — I was pleased to see that your online headline, 'Sean Penn accuses Britain of colonialism over Falklands' was accompanied by an advertisement: 'Royal Navy Now Recruiting'.

Thank you, Mr Penn.

Rod Morris (HMS *Brilliant* 1982)
Rodney Stoke, Somerset

SIR — Why would a bunch of superannuated pop singers feel that the rest of us give a tinker's toss about their views on the sovereignty of the Falkland Islands? (Or, come to think about it, their views on anything else?)

P.R.
Holcombe, Lancashire

SIR — I see that Guernsey defeated the might of Argentina at cricket today by a comfortable margin. If there is a real threat of invasion, should we send them to defend the Falklands? We need arm them only with Duckworth-Lewis.

Chris Middleton
Rotherham, South Yorkshire

SIR — Perhaps the best way of defusing all this nonsense we see in the press would be to send Prince William to Argentina. I would imagine many young Argentineans would be happy to see him if he popped over for a quick walkabout. It would certainly be cheaper than deploying warships.

David Ellis
Tarves, Aberdeenshire

AN INTERVIEW WITHOUT SANGRIA

SIR – You quote a spokesman for the Spanish Foreign Ministry requesting a 'conversation over sovereignty' of Gibraltar. A two-word conversation will suffice.

Peter Goody
Woodford Green, Essex

SIR – If the Spanish are going to be difficult over Gibraltar, is there any reason why we should contribute to bailing out Spanish banks?

Chris Lawson
High Hurstwood, East Sussex

SIR – So sorry to hear that Queen Sofia of Spain has been forbidden by the Spanish authorities to come here for the Diamond Jubilee luncheon. Is it really because of Gibraltar, or can they not afford the fare?

Alison Hodge
Kingston, East Sussex

SIR — Your correspondent suggests that we cancel our trips to Spain in return for Queen Sofia's snub to our Queen. I would never go anyway: far too many of the women sport moustaches.

Robert Warner
West Woodhay, Berkshire

SIR — I had to smile at the television coverage of the anti-austerity march in Madrid, the participants dressed in Armani tops and photographing the protest using their £500 iPads.

John Lavender
Port Erin, Isle of Man

SCANDO-NOIR

SIR — Having watched four episodes of *The Bridge* I can now see why Julian Assange doesn't want to be extradited to Sweden.

Robert Stevenson
Cheltenham, Gloucestershire

TELEVISION
AND RADIO

THE DUSTBIN CHANNEL

SIR – Can I be the only one who thinks it appropriate to have a special television channel where the likes of Jonathan Ross, Ricky Gervais, Russell Brand and Jeremy Clarkson could be consigned? We could call it the Dustbin Channel so that I, and many like-minded viewers, could more easily avoid it, along with the 900 channels on Sky.

Colin Stone
Cellardyke, Fife

SIR – The media widely refers to Jeremy Clarkson as 'one of the BBC's best exports'. So what is he still doing here?

Bharat Jashanmal
Fairford, Gloucestershire

SIR – Well, that takes the biscuit. Your reviewer suggests we watch *The Graham Norton Show*.

Richard Kellaway
Woolavington, Somerset

DON'T PANIC, BBC

SIR – I have no truck with those who say BBC programmes have not improved over the years. In the 1970s *Dad's Army* was just one of several quality programmes in the BBC schedule; now it is the best.

Ralph Griffiths
New Malden, Surrey

SIR – I think of *EastEnders* as Kafka without the laughs.

William Shepherd
Dublin

SIR – Another avenue of pleasure lost as Ceefax shuts down. In the 1990s I saw the Zimbabwean bowler Eddo Brandes take a hat-trick against England by following the match on Ceefax.

Barry McCartney
Sudbury, Suffolk

SIR – At the risk of being branded a grumpy old woman, may I ask if there is anyone out there who, like me, is driven to distraction by the interminable trailers for forthcoming programmes on the BBC? My annoyance has reached the stage that I do not watch the trailed programme on principle.

J.B.
Hailsham, East Sussex

FLEA SONG

SIR — Having watched the first half of the much heralded adaptation of *Birdsong*, I feel that those responsible should be 'done' for GBH on a novel. When the two main actors weren't staring blankly into space, they spent the rest of the time scratching around in one another's clothes, as if looking for fleas.

Pauline Kelly
Hartley, Kent

SIR — Perhaps they should rename BBC One, BBC Pornography. It is high time censorship was brought back to remove offensive content.

R.P.
Newton, Swansea

SIR — I was surprised to hear a collared dove calling in the woodland scene during the adaptation of *Birdsong*. Collared doves only started breeding in France in 1952; until then they were a very rare visitor, normally found in towns.

Ollie Pomfret (aged 13)
Langley, Hertfordshire

NOT SO ELEMENTARY, WATSON

SIR – My wife and I watched the first of the BBC's new *Sherlock* series on Sunday night, but we were both thoroughly confused by the plot. Had we blinked, simultaneously, at some crucial point? And no, we had had only one small glass of mulled wine each.

Ross Bourne
Salisbury

EUROVISION WITHDRAWAL

SIR – In the light of this country's ambivalent attitude towards membership of Europe, will Engelbert Humperdinck be representing the United Kingdom in the Eurovision Song Contest with a rendition of his classic hit 'Please Release Me, Let Me Go'?

Hugo James
Royal Wootton Bassett, Wiltshire

SIR – If Scotland gains independence, will they vote for our Eurovision entry? Otherwise, what is the point?

Brian Christley
Abergele, Conwy

SIR — Now that Engelbert Humperdinck has been superseded in age by the Russian Buranovo Grannies, is it not time to prise Sir Terence Wogan from retirement to oversee proceedings?

Peter Raw
Compton Down, Hampshire

VALUING ABU QATADA

SIR — In view of the BBC's latest manifestation of absurd political correctness — namely telling its journalists not to call Abu Qatada 'an extremist' — I would like to take this opportunity to make my own 'value judgment'. Am I alone in thinking that Abu Qatada is an obese, rebarbative extremist, and that the BBC is bringing hypocrisy into disrepute?

Tim Tawney
Hildenborough, Kent

SIR — What next for Abu Qatada? A knighthood, perhaps?

Michael Fabb
Hungerford, Berkshire

SIR — A simple, cost-effective solution to the Abu Qatada conundrum would be to call in Mossad and, for a reasonable fee, eliminate the problem.

David G. Ford
Hove, East Sussex

SIR – Why can't we extradite the Home Office instead?

Simon Shneerson
Chorleywood, Hertfordshire

SIR – I cannot understand why Abu Qatada is kicking up such a stink about returning to Jordan. I have just returned from a fortnight there and had a wonderful time. Lovely five-star hotels, delicious food, wonderful sights, friendly people – and I didn't see one drop of rain.

Charles Garth
Ampthill, Bedfordshire

DIRECTOR GENERAL SUSPENSE

SIR – I trust that any future Director General of the BBC will, if male, wear a tie with a suit, grow either a proper beard or shave daily and, if playing football, not pull his socks over his knees unless wearing a suspender belt.

Derek Lyon
Barrow-in-Furness, Cumbria

SIR – I would advocate Joey Barton. He appears to have an opinion on everything, although I doubt he would be comfortable with a reduction from his current £4 million salary.

J.P. Davis
Elstead, Surrey

BBC'S WIND FARM CRUSADE

SIR – I cannot be the only person to have noticed that the BBC is showing wind farms in background shots to so many programmes, the latest being *The Crusades* last night.

Brainwashing? Yes, get used to it, is the message.

Eileen Armstrong
Tunbridge Wells, Kent

SIR – The Bishop of Bradford asks why there is no Religious Editor at the BBC. I note there isn't a UFO Editor either. Should I complain?

Steve Cattell
Hougham, Lincolnshire

AUSTERITY AT THE BBC

SIR – The Government's austerity measures are clearly beginning to take effect. George Alagiah has had to wear the same suit twice in the past month.

Derek Smith
Sibford Gower, Oxfordshire

SIR – I recently watched, by accident, a programme called *Baking Made Easy*. When the credits were rolling, I counted that it took, give or take, 32 people to produce it. I lost interest after the name of the 'Deputy Lemon Zest Assistant' flashed by.

Should we be surprised that our licence money does not go as far as it should?

David Owen
Eldwick, West Yorkshire

SIR – I have been watching *Great British Menu* on the BBC and would not want to eat any of the dishes I have seen prepared, let alone pay for them. What is 'cooking' becoming?

J.J. Armstrong
Peacehaven, East Sussex

SIR – Please will the BBC invest in some handcuffs and ankle clamps for their television reporters to prevent them walking towards the camera and gesticulating with their hands while talking.

David Hartridge
Groby, Leicestershire

SIR – Does Jeremy Paxman wash his one outfit between each instalment of *Empire* or does he travel with several sets of the same outfit? I do wish he would change his shirt as I find myself mulling over these questions when I should be paying full attention to the programme.

Veronica Copley
London SE23

SIR – Am I alone in thinking that Jeremy Paxman looks like a proboscis monkey?

Michael Powell
Tealby, Lincolnshire

THE SPECIAL RELATIONSHIP WHERE YOU ARE

SIR – Following the main news on BBC One comes the local news or 'The News Where You Are', which we refer to as 'The Bimbo Break'. This usually brings a young woman so weighed down with lip gloss that she appears to be dribbling.

To make matters more irritating, while all news reporters are given their full names by her, the weather man is only ever introduced by his first name, as in, 'And here's Peter with the weather.'

We have to wonder, is there some special relationship here?

Tony Knight
London SE3

SIR – I'm not going to mention names (they know who they are), but what is it about working at the BBC that causes so many female newsreaders and weathergirls to lose their bust? Is it hunger, lack of sleep, low wages, over-exertion or just plain old worry about a possible move to Salford?

Joseph G. Dawson
Withnell, Lancashire

SIR – Why are weather presenters needed at all? They take up a third of the screen and usually stand blocking off Cornwall, where I live. Why not use a voice over?

Barrie Yelland
Helston, Cornwall

SIR – I'd like to forbid documentary presenters
from appearing more than once in each programme,
except perhaps fleetingly for scale.

Margaret Barrett
Market Bosworth, Leicestershire

ANALOGUE ANARCHY

SIR – Will I be the only person shedding a tear at the
loss of analogue television next month? I understand
that the new digital system varies with each make
of receiver, so your news might be a second or two
before mine.

Is accuracy no longer of value? Will we have
to forfeit punctuality? Will 'near enough' be de
rigueur?

Yours sadly,
Stanford Allen
London NW11

DR LIVINGSTONE, I PRESUME

SIR – Why does the BBC wish to render inaudible
the spoken content of their programmes?

Yesterday evening I sat, G&T in hand, to watch a
programme about Dr Livingstone in Africa. For the
first eight minutes I could not hear the commentary

as it was drowned out by background noise. I had to leave the room or I might have thrown my glass at the set or suffered a heart attack. Later my wife muted the sound and turned on the subtitles.

Rodney Savage
Henbury, Cheshire

SIR – I decided to turn on the subtitles for Brian Cox's eagerly awaited *Stargazing Live* so I wouldn't miss anything. I couldn't believe the rubbish that was being printed. I can only assume one of our recent semi-illiterate graduates had been put in charge.

Hilary Beck-Burridge
Fawley, Oxfordshire

SIR – As a self-confessed Luddite, I have inadvertently installed subtitles on my television and have failed to remove them. However, they have now become such a source of amusement during live programmes that I am tempted to remove the sound altogether.

B.H.
Hurstpierpoint, West Sussex

ARTISTIC SILENCE

SIR – I wonder whether *The Artist* could be used as a template for women's tennis matches?

Graham Bond
North Weald, Essex

SIR – If we are returning to silent films such as *The Artist*, can we also look forward to silent commercials?

Elizabeth Cleal
Freeland, Oxfordshire

SIR – That the *Downton Abbey* Christmas special was the most recorded programme ever is no surprise. It was wonderful to be able to fast-forward through those interminable adverts.

Peter Hyde
Hamble, Hampshire

SIR – Is it wrong of me to be amused that Julian Fellowes' production of *Titanic* is already known as *Drownton*?

J. Bardey
Kineton, Warwickshire

SIR – Whenever one watches a television drama, rarely does one spot males of any proper height.

A recent picture of the *Downton Abbey* cast, in which everyone is the same size, is a prime example. Does this indicate that those of us who are six feet tall or more stand very little chance of a career on the screen? Or perhaps we can look forward to a career on radio?

David Culm
Littleover, Derbyshire

RADIO ON THE MOVE

SIR – Am I the only person in Britain still playing cassettes on a much-prized portable radio/cassette player? This irreplaceable gadget also provides the only way I know to listen to radio on the move, rather than retrospectively, following some complicated, technical downloading procedure.

I live in hope that both it and the current broadcasting system will continue to survive.

Jessica Houdret
Farnham Royal, Buckinghamshire

SIR – Joan Bakewell raises the subject of accents on the radio. Surely the important factor is the thickness of the accent, rather than its origin? Neil Nunes on Radio 4 irritates me not because he has a Jamaican accent, but because it is pronounced, and delivered in a rumbling basso profundo that sets the crockery trembling.

Richard Cheeseman
Yateley, Hampshire

FLY ME TO THE OFF SWITCH

SIR – Two things the radio off-switch was invented for: *The Archers* and Frank Sinatra.

S. Lawton
Kirtlington, Oxfordshire

SIR – Your correspondents seem to be completely missing the point of *The Archers*. It's because it is inane and full of banality that we tune in. How reassuring to see that, in today's world of unrealistic soap opera drama, there is a little village out there suffering the same day-to-day problems as us ordinary mortals. How often my head nods in sympathy and agreement at the issues played out.

N.B.
Brockenhurst, Hampshire

NO TODAY, TODAY

SIR – What bliss the last six weeks have been. For Lent, my wife persuaded me to suspend a lifelong addiction to the *Today* programme. No breakfasts spoiled by the smug and arrogant John and James; the self-regarding Justin and Evan; the shrill Sarah and Caroline – all overriding their interviewees and belligerently peddling their own right-on views.

To all those who find themselves inexplicably tense and upset, I recommend a trial period of abstinence. There will be no going back for me.

Michael Tyce
Waterstock, Oxfordshire

SIR – Evan Davis, an atheist, suggests that the *Today* programme's 'Thought for the Day' slot should include contributions from spiritually minded secularists because it was 'discriminating against the non-religious'.

On a similar basis, why not include contributions from spiritually minded secularists on *Songs of Praise*? It would make a pleasant change to hear a hearty rendition of 'Guide me, O thou great broad-based diverse and inclusive values system, learner in this brownfield site'.

Ann Farmer
Woodford Green, Essex

BUSH HOUSE IN THE BUSH

SIR – When I worked in the newsroom of the BBC
World Service 40 years ago there was an interesting
– possibly apocryphal – story doing the rounds.
One of our reporters in the most remote part of
Africa came across a tribe speaking beautiful English.
Curiously they ended each sentence with a loud
whistle. Asked to explain, they said that they listened
every day to World Service, on shortwave radio.

Philip Moger
East Preston, West Sussex

DEAR DAILY TELEGRAPH

THE DAILY DEATH

SIR – Your online link to the Obituaries used to be under the News tab. It has now disappeared. How am I supposed to know if I have died or not?

Hywel ap Rees
Oakland, California

SIR – Your obituary of Lord Foley says that Queen Anne revived the family title in 1776. But who had revived Queen Anne?

Geoffrey Plowden
London W2

SIR – It is very much to be hoped that Viscount Linley is not Prince Philip's grandson, as you report today.

Rev. Richard Haggis
Littlemore, Oxfordshire

SIR – My husband's pithy summary of today's *Telegraph* was: 'Bosoms; *Downton Abbey*; and the next thing that's going to kill me.'

Val Woollven
Horrabridge, Devon

SIR – According to today's front page article, 'eating steak increases the risk of dying by 12 per cent'. Am

I now to assume that I have a 112 per cent chance of dying?

Phil Gibson
Ipswich, Suffolk

SIR – Those concerned about the latest food scare may take comfort from Jerome K. Jerome's doctor's advice in *Three Men in a Boat:* '1 lb beefsteak, with 1 pt bitter beer every 6 hours. 1 ten-mile walk every morning. 1 bed at 11 sharp every night. And don't stuff up your head with things you don't understand.'

John Sutherland
Uxbridge, Middlesex

THE DAILY TIPPLE

SIR – It is interesting to note in the reprint of the *Telegraph* from 1952 that the newspaper's price was 2d, while a bottle of Grant's Standfast Whisky was advertised at 35s. Today's paper at £1.20 is 144 times as expensive, while a bottle of Grant's Standfast at £79.95 on the internet is only 50.57 times as dear.

Is today's *Telegraph* too expensive or the whisky too cheap?

John Prichard
Claygate, Surrey

SIR – Having paid £2 for my Saturday paper,
I was irritated to find the occasional news item
interrupting my enjoyment of page after page of
advertisements.

M.G. Davis
Stockbridge, Hampshire

SIR – I am sure many of your readers will have
enjoyed the 'Journeys by Private Jet' supplement
delivered with this Saturday's *Telegraph*. However, on
the assumption that you won't be doing a 'Journeys
by Easyjet' supplement any time soon for us lesser
mortals, maybe the time has come for me to
downgrade to a tabloid on Saturdays.

Keith Martin
Cothelstone, Somerset

SIR – A 20 per cent price increase? I'm switching.
What does the *Telegraph* think it is? An energy
company?

Andrew J. Chamberlin
Plungar, Nottinghamshire

SIR, FROM MA'AM

SIR – During January I kept a record of letters
published in the *Telegraph*, which shows that

approximately 403 were written by men and 73 by women. Would this be because men write better letters? Or perhaps women have something better to do? I can't imagine it is because women have nothing to say.

Fay Davies
Barnet, Hertfordshire

SIR — My wife frequently threatens to write to the *Telegraph* about small items of news that irritate her. She never gets round to it. She is annoyed again today and intends to complain to you. She won't. I promised I would write on her behalf while she is out shopping, but unfortunately I have forgotten what it was that irritated her (there is too much choice).

However, I am sure we will both feel better now that pen has been put to paper.

John Hardy Clarke
Caythorpe, Lincolnshire

SIR — My husband is of the opinion that letters from men concern serious topics, whereas women tend to write about trivia and should, therefore, stick to the *Daily Mail*.

Christine Skeer
Sale, Cheshire

SIR – You published a letter from our headmistress yesterday saying that the most popular A-level subjects at St Swithun's School are chemistry, maths and biology.

Does it not occur to her that perhaps the sixth-form pupils only wish to study these subjects in order to understand the process of home-distilling alcohol, recognise how to conduct a shopping budget and to familiarise ourselves with the process of producing children in our married life?

A sixth-form pupil
St Swithun's School, Winchester

AN UPDATE FROM FLORENCE

SIR – Last year I wrote to you regarding my 15-year-old goldfish, Florence, and asked how long I could realistically expect her to carry on before she hung up her fins. You very kindly published my letter, even accompanying it with a picture of some beautiful fish that didn't resemble Florence at all.

I am now writing with the very sad news that Florence has recently passed away. Quite frankly, I think the fame went to her head and she could not cope with her celebrity status.

Catherine Kidson
Bradfield, Berkshire

SIR — Why is it that readers surface with some bizarre topic for print, whereupon a debate on the subject rages for a good three weeks until the next topic takes its place?

I bet if I suggested that square pancakes were better than round crêpes, it would start the pens quivering.

On second thoughts it won't — just to spite me.

Derek Taylor
Maplehurst, West Sussex

SIR — I know that spring is on its way when I start to read letters about spring being on its way in the *Telegraph*.

Peter Mansion
Blockley, Gloucestershire

RANK PREJUDICE

SIR — As a Lieutenant-Commander on the Retired List of the Royal Navy, I consider that the Lieutenant-Commander on page 19 of today's newspaper should be thoroughly ashamed of his sloppy salute.

J.M. Gawley
Havant, Hampshire

SIR – I'm a little tired of seeing letters signed by Air Commodore This (retd); Captain That RN (retd); and General Other (retd). Please ask them to desist.

Pilot Officer M.B.P. (retd)
Bristol

SIR – Could you please ban letters with more than one signatory?

John de Lange (and 25,000 others)
London N12

SIR – I would have given the contents of one of today's letters far more credibility if the first two authors had not been, respectively, a self-confessed Australian Marxist/anarchist and the Director of the South East England RSPB.

R.B.
Hindhead, Surrey

SIR – I notice that Keith Flett of London N17, formerly renowned as a prolific contributor to the *Guardian*'s letters page, has written a letter to *The Daily Telegraph*. I wonder if he has crossed the great divide or whether he just wants to see how the other half live.

Rob Eagle
Marlow, Buckinghamshire

SIR – I couldn't help noticing that *The Daily Telegraph* has published yet another letter from a certain reader. I am left wondering with whom I have to sleep in the letters offices to get just one of my letters published.

Oliver O'Hanlon
London SE1

SIR – For Heaven's sake, you must have better material than the ongoing ramblings of the two old farts in Edinburgh and Kent. I realise that this is too tasteless for publication, but it needs saying: my only reason for continuing to buy the *Telegraph*, political leanings aside, is to stay alive long enough to read their obituaries.

B.A.E.
Norwich

SIR – I find more pure wisdom in the letters columns than I do in the rest of your paper. Think of the extra profit you would make by sacking your permanent staff and inviting correspondents to fill the gaps.

J. Roger Bell
Lymington, Hampshire

SIR – If there was a political party for the Disgusted of Tunbridge Wells, I would be one of the first to join.

June Mundell
Castle Cary, Somerset

TEAM TELEGRAPH

SIR – After reading successive articles by Boris Johnson, Dr John Sentamu and the saintly Charles Moore in yesterday's *Telegraph*, I experienced what I can only describe as a brief moment of bliss: I imagined a country in which these three titans of our age were Prime Minister, Archbishop of Canterbury and Director General of the BBC. It wouldn't even have to be in that order.

Kevin Cunliffe
Prestbury, Cheshire

SIR – I do look forward to Boris Johnson's Monday rants, and generally find myself in agreement; I'm not sure, however, that I agree entirely with his assertion in today's piece that jumping in the river 'didn't do him much harm'.

Bharat Jashanmal
Fairford, Gloucestershire

SIR – If today's brilliant Matt cartoon doesn't warrant a knighthood for Matt there is no justice in the world.

David Simpson
Marlow, Buckinghamshire

SIR – While I always appreciate the thoroughness of Victoria Moore's wine recommendations, this week I find myself more eager to know: where did she get that beautiful dress?

Therese Beckwith
London SW1

SIR – I would be most grateful if you could ask James Delingpole to put his shirt back on. He is not 'all that'.

Sally Jaspars
Aberdeen

STRIPPED AWAY

SIR – You report that Alex is 'away for a bit'. Would it be indelicate to ask, 'for a bit of what?'

Patrick Thomas
Over Wallop, Hampshire

SIR – We were told that Alex is away until 3 September. Today this has been changed to 'staying out of public view'. My guess is that he has been arrested as a prime mover behind this Libor business and, even as I write, is singing like a canary.

Poor old Clive hasn't a chance.

Derek Jenkins
Camberley, Surrey

READ IT AND WEEP

SIR – Every morning I sit down with the *Telegraph* and my eyes weep. Is this because of the depressing news, or does the paper emit irritating fumes? Does anyone else have this problem? Or is it just me?

Anthony Goddard
Newton Harcourt, Leicestershire

LOOKING A MILLION POUNDS

SIR – After staring for some time at Mark Rothko's 'Untitled' in today's *Telegraph*, wondering why on earth anyone would think this daub worth £50 million, a moment of sublime revelation came to me. Oh, so clever! I could now see the face of a beautiful woman appear within the orange haze. What subtlety! The image even reminded me of the Prime Minister's wife.

I then discovered that this was in fact a photograph of Samantha Cameron shining through from the page behind.

William Geddes
Macclesfield, Cheshire

SIR – My newspaper, when viewed from across the room, appears to show a picture of the Queen, the Duchess of Cornwall and the Duchess of Cambridge above the headline: 'Witchcraft threat to children'. Is this another *Telegraph* investigation we have yet to hear about?

Edward King
Grittleton, Wiltshire

SIR – How refreshing to hear the latest news on the reclusive actress Dame Helen Mirren.

Michael Powell
Tealby, Lincolnshire

SIR – Could someone please explain to me why the *Telegraph* appears to have an obsession with Gwyneth Paltrow? This week she features in the education section for no apparent reason. Could you try to have several weeks before mentioning her again?

Peter Mobbs
Llanfairfechan, Conwy

SIR – Albert Einstein did most of his foundational work as a 23-year-old. Why then do the media always publish a photo of him in his dotage (or, worse, the joke photo with his tongue sticking out)? It reinforces the 'crazy scientist' stereotype, a disastrous mistake at a time when people need to take science seriously.

There are several photos of the young Einstein available (see attached).

Mik Shaw
Goring-by-Sea, West Sussex

SIR – Any listener to *The Archers* will tell you that they know perfectly well what Tony Archer looks like, so there is no need to illustrate your articles with photos of the actor who plays him.

David Wells
London E6

BEMUSED FASHION PAGE VICTIMS

SIR – Each Wednesday I attempt to fathom what the world is coming to when I study in disbelief the prices quoted on your fashion pages. £1,495 for a jacket, euphemistically called a coat? £1,495 for a skirt? At these prices, no wonder women attempt to hide the true cost of their wardrobe from men.

I might just learn how to use a sewing machine, in order to manufacture something out of a bedspread and charge a fortune for it.

Alan Brown
Medstead, Hampshire

SIR – I am totally ignorant about women's fashion, or so my wife tells me, but that dress worn by Keira Knightley on today's front page looks as if she is wearing a pair of boxer shorts with a skirt over the top.

J.M.
Horsington, Lincolnshire

SIR – Why are all the models on the fashion pages pigeon-toed? Is this a requirement or just another new fashion?

Helen Brady
Halesowen, West Midlands

SIR – Why do I think that Karl Lagerfeld's head will fall off when he takes off his collar?

Letty Sykes
Rainham, Essex

NEVER MIND THE B****

SIR – Not a day goes by without your carrying an
item about some notable resorting to expletives. As
you always give enough clues to make the expletive
clear, why don't you just spell it out? The D***y
T*******h used to have more b***s.

Edward Bell
Sevenoaks, Kent

HILARIOUS HATCHES

SIR – Bravo, Robert Colvile, for highlighting some
of the ridiculous names bestowed on children these
days. When my husband and I want a good chuckle
we always look in the Births Announcement column.
We are rarely disappointed.

Jean Bryant
East Grinstead, West Sussex

SIR – Every day in your For Sale/Wanted section,
there is a gentleman asking for Old Havana cigars.
I wonder if he ever gets any, and if so, what he does
with them.

John Sykes
Cheadle, Staffordshire

SIR — I have been looking everywhere for a commodious bath to replace the oversized washing-up bowl that modern designers seem to think fits the bill. Any chance you could find out the make and model of the bathtub that you report held an 8ft long alligator?

Andrew M. Courtney
Hampton Wick, Middlesex

HAMPSHIRE AND THE SAHARA

SIR — I cannot possibly be the only person who is annoyed to read that Britain is hotter than another carefully selected place in the world. It is a matter of complete indifference to me.

'Hotter than the Sahara' was reported on the front page on 23 March as temperatures reached 19°C in Hampshire. However, Casablanca was 26°C, Cairo was 23°C and Tunis was 21°C.

I wonder if the newspapers in these three countries carried reports reading, 'Just hotter than Middle Wallop'.

Geoff Gibbs
Bristol

SIR — Is there any chance that we might achieve an acceptable and useful standard of weather forecasting? Last Saturday your forecast was for a high of 15°C in the London area. It proved to be only 11°C. The same thing happened on Tuesday. On both occasions I dressed for golf according to your forecast. On both occasions I was very cold.

D.T.
Brookmans Park, Hertfordshire

SIR – One of your headlines today, 'Iceberg the size of Manhattan raises fears over global warming', has left me very little the wiser. We have happily spent a lifetime with 'the size of Wales' scale. Why confuse us now?

J.B.
London W4

SIR – 52 years ago the United Kingdom changed from degrees Fahrenheit to degrees Centigrade when indicating temperature; that is with the exception of my wife and *The Daily Telegraph*. On Tuesday 13 March, the *Telegraph* used Centigrade on page 11. I don't think my wife will be so quick to change.

M.J. Andrews
Curridge, Berkshire

LIKING THE TELEGRAPH

SIR – I am currently a student in my final year at

university. Out of a friends list of 370, 66 have used the *Guardian* Facebook app in the past month alone. My news feed is dominated by lurid *Guardian* stories about self-pitying hermaphrodites.

Please provide a *Telegraph* app. Many young people are receptive to the *Telegraph*, and seek an alternative to the *Pravda* for public-sector workers.

J.B.
Southampton

SIR – While I am well aware of the need for *The Daily Telegraph* to attract new and younger readers, I am wondering how many of us more established old fogies are expected to get up – or are capable of getting up – to go running with Matt Roberts, the personal trainer to the Prime Minister?

Something gentler like tai chi, perhaps?

Richard Wyatt
Totnes, Devon

TRADITIONAL KINDLING

SIR – As a rural dweller it has been suggested to me that I might find it more convenient to subscribe to the *Telegraph* electronically. I suppose that might work in the warmer months but in the winter I rely on your traditional newspaper for lighting my log fires.

For so long as I live in a house with an open

fireplace, I will feel obliged to favour my kindling over my Kindle.

Roger Belle
Llandevaud, Gwent

SIR — In Lord Saatchi's article he refers to the term 'app' no fewer than eight times. I have no idea what 'app' stands for or means. Neither, I suspect, do many other of your readers. I wish Lord Saatchi had explained it.

Sir Jeremy Chance
Woodhall Spa, Lincolnshire

CROSS WORDS

SIR — I wish to protest at your cavalier attitude to your crossword solvers. I am fed up with you putting a whole page advertisement at the back of the paper, thus relegating the crosswords to an inferior internal position. Stop this at once. Have you no respect for the traditions and customs of your readership?

The inconvenience of yet another fold to the paper is unnecessary, especially as I believe no one looks at the advertisements anyway.

Christopher Strong
Bilborough, Nottinghamshire

SIR – For many years I have been trying to win a fountain pen by completing the Saturday Prize Crossword. I attribute my lack of success to the fact that since I complete the puzzle in biro, no one can read what I have written.

Stewart Keating
Surbiton, Surrey

SIR – Why have you moved the Mind Gym to the lower half of the page? Do you realise I no longer have a clear margin at the top of the page to allow me to scribble my calculations?

D.H.
Basingstoke, Hampshire

SIR – Please, please, may we be spared any more End of Year Quiz Competitions? Each one makes me realise how addled my brain is becoming.

Geoff Morton
March, Cambridgeshire

SIR – Having just taken my daily statins, I have now forgotten why I am writing to you.

Colin Henderson
Cranleigh, Surrey

EDITING THE EDITOR

SIR — In a very amiable review by Iain Hollingshead in yesterday's *Daily Telegraph* he makes great play of my 'sharp line in blazers'. I wore a sports jacket throughout the programme.

How can anyone fully trust a *Telegraph* man who makes this sort of mistake?

Melvyn Bragg
London WC1

PS

Dear Iain,

What an honour. Not only will my letter appear in a book, but the three men in my family are trying to figure out which of my 'disgusted of Markington' letters is to be published.

This cat has got the cream.

Linn Carter
Markington, North Yorkshire
PS Which letter is it?

Dear Iain,

I am delighted I am likely to be included in the next book of letters which didn't quite make it. Over the years in my private battle with Mike Cole of Bridgwater, Somerset, he has had far fewer letters in the paper, but has had two in the books, while I have had none until now.

I think it would be nice if, after a qualifying number of published letters, contributors received a tie, or a brooch for the ladies. They would make wonderful conversation openers. It would also add to my collection of 80 or so ties.

Chris Harding
Parkstone, Dorset

Dear Iain,

Greetings from Over Wallop, and thank you for your note. Delighted! Amazing how Letters to the Editor act as a social networking site. Among the correspondents have been my wife's bridesmaid, a Royal Air Force flying instructor of many years ago, a couple of generals from a distant and long-forgotten desert war and even my son.

One notes the absence of regular contributors and the obvious conclusion is drawn. This absence has added a touch of nostalgia to the presence in the kitchen of a particularly huge pepper mill.

When studied in conjunction with the Obituary Pages and Books, one sees a wonderful pattern of life in the Letters pages.

Patrick Thomas
Over Wallop, Hampshire